RENAL DIET COOKBOOK FOR BEGINNERS

A Comprehensive Guide With 300 Low Sodium, Potassium, and Phosphorus Mouthwatering Recipes for Every Stage of Disease to Improve Kidney Function and Avoid Dialysis.

Written By

Delilah Hooper

Table of Contents

Chapter 8: Desserts Recipes 107

Chapter 9: Smoothies and Drinks 125

Introduction

Despite their tiny size, the kidneys perform a number of functions which are vital for the body to be able to function healthily.

These include:

- Filtering excess fluids and waste from the blood
- Creating the enzyme known as renin which regulates blood pressure
- Ensuring bone marrow creates red blood cells
- Controlling calcium and phosphorus levels through absorption and excretion

Unfortunately, when kidney disease reaches a chronic stage, these functions start to stop working. However, with the right treatment and lifestyle, it is possible to manage symptoms and continue living well. This is even more applicable in the earlier stages of the disease. Tactlessly, 10% of all adults over the age of 20 will experience some form of kidney disease in their lifetime. There are a variety of different treatments for kidney disease, which depend on the cause of the disease.

Possible causes are outlined below:

- DIABETES: In the United States and other countries where the 'Standard American Diet' runs rampant, the number one leading cause of kidney disease is high blood pressure and Type 2 diabetes. Both of these diseases are either completely preventable or at least treatable and once the root issue has been treated, kidney disease issues can also dissipate.

- GLOMERULONEPHRITIS: Damage to the glomeruli (the filters in your kidneys), impairs the kidneys' ability to filter waste materials. This can be caused by damage to the immune system and if this is the case, can be treated with medication. It is either experienced for a short period of time (acute glomerulonephritis), or for a longer period of time (chronic). In chronic cases, further problems can arise such as high blood pressure, organ damage and later chronic kidney disease.

- ACUTE RENAL FAILURE/ACUTE KIDNEY INJURY: Sudden damage or failure of the kidney can be caused by a rapid loss of blood to the kidneys, sepsis or even severe dehydration. Infection, poison and some medicines are also known to lead to acute kidney issues.

- SUDDEN BLOCKAGE: Kidney stones, tumors, injuries and an enlarged prostate in men can stop urine from passing through the kidneys as it should. This can cause swelling in the lower extremities, a loss of appetite, vomiting or nausea, extreme tiredness, restlessness, feelings of confusion, or even an acute pain beneath the ribs (known as flank pain).

- ECLAMPSIA: This can be experienced during pregnancy when the placenta doesn't function as it should do, creating high blood pressure and sometimes leading to kidney problems.

- BREAKDOWN OF MUSCLE TISSUE: Under extreme pressure, for example when running a marathon or undergoing other feats of massive exertion, the body starts to break down muscle tissue after it has used all other available fuel. If this continues unchecked, too much of the protein known as myoglobin will ultimately end up in the bloodstream, putting undue strain on the kidneys and potentially leading to further implications.

- IMMUNE SYSTEM: Common immune system diseases that can lead to kidney issues include lupus, hepatitis C, hepatitis B, HIV, and aids. These can lead to what is known as chronic kidney disease (any form of kidney disease that lasts for three months or longer). Sometimes the sufferer of the immune disease will not experience the symptoms of the kidney disease until it reaches a chronic stage; this can be dangerous as it is a lot harder to manage once it has reached this level.

- EXTREME URINARY TRACT INFECTIONS: Urinary tract infections that occur within the kidneys rather than the bladder are known as pyelonephritis and occur when a traditional urinary tract infection remains untreated long enough for it to spread into the upper urinary tract system. This can cause scarring in the kidneys which can lead to severe flaws in kidney functioning.

- STREPTOCOCCAL INFECTIONS: Commonly known as a strep infection, this bacterium can infect the throat as well as various layers of the skin, the middle ear, the sinuses or even in a more severe case, a widespread vicious rash known as scarlet fever. This bacterium is known to result in the glomeruli (individual filters in the kidneys) becoming infected.

- POLYCYSTIC KIDNEY DISEASE: This type of kidney disease is typically passed down from parent to child and causes cysts filled with fluid to form on the kidneys themselves.

- BIRTH DEFECTS: Depending on the severity of the defect, kidney disease could form simply because the kidneys do not function correctly or because of an obstruction in the urinary tract before birth.

Chapter 1: Kidney Disease and Diet

What is Chronic Kidney Disease (CKD)?

There is chronic kidney disease (CKD) when it is damaged kidneys or kidney function decline for three months or more. There are five stages of evolution of a CRM according to the severity of the renal involvement or the degree of deterioration of its function.

Sometimes the kidney failure suddenly occurs. In this case, it is called an acute failure of the kidney. An injury, infection, or something else may be the cause. Acute renal failure is often treated with urgency by dialysis for some time. Often, kidney function recovers itself. Generally, this disease settles slowly and silently, but it progresses over the years. People with CKD do not necessarily go from stage 1 to stage 5 of the disease. Stage 5 of the disease is known under the name of end stage renal disease (ESRD) or kidney failure in the final stage.

It is essential to know that the expressions terminal, final, and ultimate mean the end of any function of the kidneys (kidneys working at less than 15% of their standard capacity) and not the end of your life. To stay alive at this stage of the disease, it is necessary to resort to dialysis or a kidney transplant. Dialysis and transplantation are known as renal replacement therapy (TRS). This means that dialysis or the transplanted kidney will "supplement" or "replace" the sick kidneys and do their job.

What Are the Causes of Chronic Kidney Disease?

There are different kinds of diseases and disorders of the kidneys. At present, we do not know for sure all the causes. Some are hereditary, while others develop with age. They are often associated with another disease, such as diabetes, heart disease, or high blood pressure.

Most kidney diseases attack kidney filters, damaging their ability to eliminate waste and excess fluids. For the moment, no treatment can cure these diseases, but it is possible to prevent them or to slow down their evolution. This is especially true of diseases such as diabetes and hypertension, the leading causes of kidney failure.

Who Runs the Risk of Having a CKD?

Even though people with diabetes use insulin by injection or take medication, they are not able to shelter the lesion of some small blood vessels, like those in the retina of the eye. In this case, the retina may be damaged, resulting in loss of vision. Also, they are not immune to the deterioration of the fragile blood vessels of the renal filters.

Progressive deterioration of the kidneys is seen when urine tests show higher and higher protein levels. As the disease progresses, the number of protein increases. As for treatment, the sooner it starts (for example, with drugs such as ACE inhibitors or A2 blocking agents), the more likely it is to slow the progression of the disease. Kidney disease caused by diabetes can slow the evolution of the disease regardless of its stage.

Over time, diabetes can reach kidney filters at a point of no return: the kidneys no longer function, and renal replacement therapy becomes essential. People with diabetes are prone to infections, which are changing rapidly. If these infections, especially those of the urinary tract, are not treated, they can damage the kidneys. It is recommended that people with diabetes not overlook any infection and have it treated immediately.

Hypertension

The kidneys secrete a hormone that plays an essential role in increasing or reducing blood pressure. When the kidneys are so affected that they do not function properly, the secretion of this hormone can increase and cause hypertension, which in turn, damages the kidneys. It is, therefore, necessary to closely monitor hypertension to avoid the deterioration of renal function in the long term.

Glomerulonephritis

The glomerulonephritis, or nephritis, declares when glomeruli, these little tiny filters used to purify the blood, deteriorates. There are several kinds of glomerulonephritis. Some are hereditary, while others occur as a result of certain diseases such as strep throat. The causes of most glomerulonephritis are not yet known. Some glomerulonephritis cure without medical treatment, while others require prescription drugs. Some do not respond to any treatment and who have chronic kidney disease. Some clues suggest that glomerulonephritis is due to a deficiency in the immune system of the body.

Autosomal Dominant Polycystic Disease

Often in their forties, people with the disease will need dialysis or kidney transplant. But because the loss of kidney function is changing at a different pace, depending on the individual, the time between the onset of cysts and the need for dialysis varies widely. Since the disease is hereditary, people are advised to inform other family members to carry out the required tests as they too may be affected.

The Obstruction of the Urinary Tract

Any obstruction (or blockage) of the urinary tract may damage the kidneys. Obstructions can occur in the ureter or at the end of the bladder. Narrowing of the ureter at the superior or inferior level is sometimes due to congenital malformations, which sometimes leads to chronic kidney disease in children. In adults, increased prostate volume, kidney stones, or tumors often obstruct the urinary tract.

Reflux Nephropathy

The reflux nephropathy is the new name of the former "chronic pyelonephritis."

Illegal Drugs

The use of illegal drugs can cause kidney damage. Over-the-counter medications (without a prescription) High-dose and long-term use of over-the-counter medications can cause kidney damage. Important: Beware of medications, including herbal remedies, sold without a prescription. It would be wiser to seek the advice of your doctor before buying them.

Prescription Drugs

Some medications prescribed to people with kidney disease cause renal dysfunction. The lesions are sometimes reversible and sometimes irreversible. Many medications prescribed by prescription are safe but provided the doctor makes changes accurate to the dosage. So always ask your doctor or your pharmacist, information about potential side effects of prescribed drugs.

Other Kidney Disorders

Other issues can affect the kidneys, such as, for example, kidney stones, Syndrome Alport, Fabry disease, Wilms tumor (children only), not including infections of bacterial origin.

What Are the Symptoms of Kidney Disease?

In chronic kidney disease, the deterioration of kidney function is gradual. At the very beginning of the CKD, there are hardly any warning signs or apparent symptoms. In some cases, it is difficult to detect any evidence while the kidneys are already severely affected. Laboratory analysis of proteins and blood in the urine (urine analysis) can show at an early stage whether the kidney is affected or not. The calculation of serum creatinine levels makes it possible to know, well before other signs occur, whether the kidneys function well or not, or whether there is a decrease in renal function.

Warning signs or symptoms of kidney disease:

- High blood pressure
- The swelling of the eyes, hands, and feet
- Blood in the urine, cloudy or dark urine such as tea
- The presence of proteins in the urine
- Urines foamier than normal
- The frequent urge to urinate during the night
- Less urine or difficulty urinating
- Fatigue, difficulty concentrating
- Loss of appetite or weight
- Generalized and persistent itching

The Uremia

"Uremia" is a word that comes from the Greek word meaning Urine in the blood. The uremia declares when the kidneys no longer function usually and are no longer able to remove waste from the body. Many symptoms of uremia occur when kidney function deteriorates.

This varies from person to person, but in most of them, the symptoms occur when the kidneys are functioning at less than 20 - 30% of their average capacity. The more the kidney function is degraded, the more waste accumulates in the blood. Symptoms may worsen and may include shortness of breath, nausea, vomiting, itching, and headache.

Also, high blood pressure, anemia, or increased levels of acid and potassium in the blood may cause even more severe problems. Even before the worsening of the uremia, you may be prescribed dialysis or grafting.

Warning signs or possible symptoms of uremia:

- Weight loss
- Memory problems
- Tiredness
- Leg cramps
- Weakness
- The insomnia
- Nausea
- Itches
- Vomiting
- The intolerance to cold
- A bad feeling
- Chest pain taste in the mouth
- A yellowish color or brownish skin
- Lack of appetite
- The shaking of the legs
- A decrease in sexual desire
- The shortness of breath
- Bruising tendencies

What Can Be Done to Prevent the Evolution of a CKD?

The chronic renal disease does not necessarily make it to end-stage renal failure. There are some options to help possibly prevent or even decrease the rate of your progress. By adopting healthy habits, many people with CKDs have a better quality of life. Well-being is a complete physical, mental, and social state. Ask the members of your health care team to explain how to strive for wellness and adopt principles such as:

- A well-balanced diet
- Physical activities at regular intervals (ideally 45 to 60 minutes four to five times a week)
- Well-controlled blood pressure
- Balanced blood glucose (in the presence of diabetes)
- Stop smoking
- Control of anemia (maintenance of a normal blood count)
- Maintaining a healthy weight
- Moderation in alcohol consumption (maximum of two drinks per day)
- Taking medication according to the doctor's instructions
- It is also essential to be familiar with your kidney disease and to listen to the information and advice given to you from your doctor and medical care team.

Chapter 2: The Renal Diet Explained

The Benefits

The Renal diet controls your consumption of sodium, protein, potassium and phosphorous. A renal diet contributes to preventing renal failure. Below are a list of food/nutrients you should avoid preventing kidney related problems:

Phosphate: Consumption of phosphate becomes dangerous when kidney failure reaches 80% and goes to the 4th/5th stage of kidney failure. So, it is better to lower your phosphate intake by counting the calories and minerals.

Protein: Good source of protein are eggs, milk, cheese, meat, nuts, and fish.

Potassium: After getting diagnosed, if your results show your potassium level is high in the blood, then you should restrict your potassium intake. Baked and fried potatoes are very high in potassium. Leafy greens, fruit juices are high in potassium. You can still enjoy vegetables that are low in potassium.

Sodium: Adding salt is very important in our food, but when you are suffering from kidney problems, you have to omit or minimize your salt intake. Too much sodium intake can trigger high blood pressure and fluid retention in the body. You need to find substitutes that help season your food. Herbs and spices that are extracted from plants are a good option. Using garlic, pepper, mustard can increase the taste of your food without adding any salt. Avoid artificial "salts" that are low in sodium because they are high in potassium, which is also dangerous for kidney health.

Renal diets help people with kidney disease increase their quality of life.

Other types of food may be harmful to kidneys infected with a disease, so you need to make sure you have a sound knowledge of the infection and how it affects the body. You don't want kidney disease, but there are ways to boost your well-being by changing your diet. In reality, renal diets help you manage your health and reduce kidney disease.

Nutrients You Need

Potassium
Potassium is a naturally occurring mineral found in nearly all foods, in varying amounts. Our bodies need an amount of potassium to help with muscle activity as well as electrolyte balance and regulation of blood pressure. However, if potassium is in excess within the system and the kidneys can't expel it (due to renal disease), fluid retention and muscle spasms can occur.

Phosphorus
Phosphorus is a trace mineral found in a wide range of foods and especially dairy, meat, and eggs. It acts synergistic ally with calcium as well as Vitamin D to promote bone health. However, when there is damage in the kidneys, excess amounts of the mineral cannot be taken out and this can cause bone weakness.

Calories
When being on a renal diet, it is vital to give yourself the right number of calories to fuel your system. The exact number of calories you should consume daily depends on your age, gender, general health status and stage of renal disease. In most cases though, there are no strict limitations in the calorie intake, as long as you take them from proper sources that are low in sodium, potassium, and phosphorus. In general, doctors recommend a daily limit between 1800-2100 calories per day to keep weight within the normal range.

Protein
Protein is an essential nutrient that our systems need to develop and generate new connective tissue e.g. muscles, even during injuries. Protein also helps stop bleeding and supports the immune system fight infections. A healthy adult with no kidney disease would usually need 40-65 grams of protein per day.

However, in renal diet, protein consumption is a tricky subject as too much or too little can cause problems. Protein, when being metabolized by our systems also creates waste which is typically processed by the kidneys. But when kidneys are damaged or underperforming, as in the case of kidney disease that waste will stay in the system. This is why patients in more advanced CKD stages are advised to limit their protein consumption as well.

Fats
Our systems need fats and particularly good fats as a fuel source and for other metabolic cell functions. A diet rich in bad and trans or saturated fats though can significantly raise the odds of developing heart problems, which often occur with the renal disease. This is why most physicians advise their renal patients to follow a diet that contains a decent amount of good fats and a meager amount of trans (processed) or saturated fat.

Sodium

Sodium is an essential mineral that our bodies need to regulate fluid and electrolyte balance. It also plays a role in normal cell division in the muscles and nervous system. However, in kidney disease, sodium can quickly spike at higher than normal levels and the kidneys will be unable to expel it causing fluid accumulation as a side-effect. Those who also suffer from heart problems as well should limit its consumption as it may raise blood pressure.

Carbohydrates

Carbs act as a major and quick fuel source for the body's cells. When we consume carbs, our systems turn them into glucose and then into energy for "feeding" our body cells. Carbs are generally not restricted in the renal diet. Still, some types of carbs contain dietary fiber as well, which helps regulate normal colon function and protect blood vessels from damage.

Dietary Fiber

Fiber is an important element in our system that cannot be properly digested but plays a key role in the regulation of our bowel movements and blood cell protection. The fiber in the renal diet is generally encouraged as it helps loosen up the stools, relieve constipation and bloating and protect from colon damage. However, many patients don't get enough amounts of dietary fiber per day as many of them are high in potassium or phosphorus. Fortunately, there are some good dietary fiber sources for CKD patients that have lower amounts of these minerals compared to others.

Vitamins/Minerals

Our systems, according to medical research, need at least 13 vitamins and minerals to keep our cells fully active and healthy. Patients with renal disease though are more likely to be depleted by water-soluble vitamins like B-complex and Vitamin C, as a result, or limited fluid consumption. Therefore, supplementation with these vitamins along with a renal diet program should help cover any possible vitamin deficiencies. Supplementation of fat-soluble vitamins like vitamins A, K, and E may be avoided as they can quickly build up in the system and turn toxic.

Fluids

When you are in an advanced stage of renal disease, fluid can quickly build-up and lead to problems. While it is important to keep your system well hydrated, you should avoid minerals like potassium and sodium which can trigger further fluid build-up and cause a host of other symptoms.

Nutrient You Need to Avoid

Salt or sodium is known for being one of the most important ingredients that the renal diet prohibits its use. This ingredient, although simple, can badly and strongly affect your body and especially the kidneys. Any excess of sodium can't be easily filtered because of the failing condition of the kidneys. A large build-up of sodium can cause catastrophic results on your body. Potassium and Phosphorus are also prohibited for kidney patients depending on the stage of kidney disease.

The Best Advice to Avoid Dialysis

Dialysis is the artificial process that is used to clean and purify the blood outside of the kidneys. It is a long and excruciating process that most people don't care for. That is why it is suggested to control the renal damage to avoid such extreme conditions. Here are certain tips to avoid dialysis:

- Exercise regularly
- Eat right and lose excess weight
- Don't smoke
- Avoid excess salt in your diet
- Control high blood pressure
- Control diabetes
- Talk with your healthcare team

However, in the case of extreme kidney damage, dialysis remains the only option for people.

A Kidney-Friendly Lifestyle

Once a kidney is damaged there is no one-time solution or magic to undo all the damage. It requires constant management and a whole new lifestyle to provide a healthy environment for your kidneys.

For healthy kidneys, you just need to keep the following in mind:

- ✓ Upgrade your vegetable intake to 5–9 vegetables per day.
- ✓ Reduce the salt intake in your diet.
- ✓ Cut down the overall protein intake.
- ✓ Remove all the triggers of heart diseases, like fats and sugar, from your diet.
- ✓ Do not consume pesticides and other environmental contaminants.
- ✓ Try to consume fresh food; homemade is the best.
- ✓ Avoid using food additives, as they contain high amounts of potassium, sodium, and phosphorous.
- ✓ Drink lots of sodium-free drinks, especially water.
- ✓ Choose to be more active and exercise regularly.
- ✓ Do not smoke to avoid toxicity.
- ✓ Obesity can create a greater risk of kidney diseases, so control your weight.
- ✓ Do not take painkillers excessively, such as Ibuprofen, as they can also damage your kidneys.

Chapter 3: Shopping List and Meal Plan

Shopping List for Week 1

Fruits and Vegetables
Apples (2)
Blueberries (8 ounces)
Cabbage, green, shredded (½ cup)
Carrots (4)
Celery stalks (7)
Corn, frozen kernels (2 cups)
Cucumbers, English (2)
Garlic (16 cloves, or 9 teaspoons minced and 4 cloves)
Jalapeño pepper (1)
Lemons (4)
Lettuce, Boston (1 head)
Limes (4)
Onions, sweet (5)
Peppers, bell, red (2)
Scallions (4)
Snow peas (½ cup)
Sprouts, bean (½ cup)

Dairy and Dairy Alternatives
Butter, unsalted (¾ cup)
Cheese, cream, plain (5 ounces)
Cheese, Parmesan, low-fat (1 ounce)
Eggs (18 eggs)
Milk, coconut (¼ cup)
Milk, unsweetened rice (4½ cups)
Milk, vanilla, rice, not enriched (1¼ cups)
Sour cream, light (2 tablespoons)

Spices and Herbs
Basil, fresh (2 bunches)
Bay leaves, dried (4)
Cardamon, ground
Cayenne pepper
Chinese five-spice powder
Chives, fresh (1 bunch)
Cilantro, fresh (1 bunch)
Cinnamon, ground
Cloves, ground
Coriander, ground
Cumin, ground
Curry powder
Dill, fresh (1 bunch)
Fennel powder
Ginger, fresh (2-inch piece)
Ginger, ground
Green chili powder
Mustard, ground
Nutmeg, ground
Oregano, fresh (1 bunch)
Parsley, fresh (1 bunch)
Peppercorns, black, freshly ground
Peppercorns, black
Red pepper flakes
Sage, fresh (1 bunch)
Sweet paprika, ground
Thyme, fresh (1 bunch)
Turmeric, ground

Fish and Seafood
Cod (4 fillets totaling 12 ounces)
Crab meat, queen (8 ounces)
Salmon (4 fillets totaling 12 ounces)
Shrimp (8 ounces)
Tuna, yellowfin (4 fillets totaling 12 ounces)

Meat and Poultry
Beef, tenderloin (4 steaks totaling 12 ounces)
Chicken breasts, boneless, skinless (36 ounces)
Chicken carcass, skin removed (1)
Chicken thighs, boneless, skinless (6)
Pork, top loin (4 chops totaling 12 ounces)
Turkey, ground, 93% lean (8 ounces)

Other
Baking soda substitute, Ener-G (3½ teaspoons)
Bread, Italian (2 slices)
Bread, white (8 slices)
Breadcrumbs
Buckwheat, whole (2 tablespoons)
Bulgur (½ cup)
Chickpeas (4 ounces)
Cooking spray
Couscous (2 cups)
Flour, all-purpose
Honey
Hot pepper sauce
Jam, strawberry (¼ cup)
Linguine
Oil, canola
Oil, olive
Penne
Sugar, granulated
Tortillas, flour, 6-inch diameter (2)
Vanilla extract, pure

Shopping List for Week 2

Fruits and Vegetables

Apples (2)
Blueberries (8 ounces)
Carrots (4)
Celery stalks (8)
Corn, frozen kernels (2 cups)
Cucumber, English (1)
Garlic (14 cloves or 10 teaspoons minced and 2 cloves)
Lemons (4)
Lettuce, Boston (1 head)

Limes (2)
Onions, sweet (6)
Peppers, banana (2)
Peppers, bell, red (2)
Pepper, bell, green (1)
Pepper, jalapeño (2)
Scallion (2)
Snow peas (½ cup)
Sprouts, bean (½ cup)

Dairy and Dairy Alternatives

Butter, unsalted (½ cup)
Cheese, Parmesan, low-fat (1 ounce)
Cheese, cream, plain (5 ounces)
Eggs (18)

Sour cream, light (2 tablespoons)
Milk, coconut (¼ cup)
Milk, rice, unsweetened (4 cups)
Milk, rice, vanilla (1¼ cups)

Spices and Herbs

Basil, fresh (1 bunch)
Bay leaves (2)
Black pepper
Cardamom, ground
Cayenne pepper
Chinese five-spice powder
Chives, fresh (1 bunch)
Cilantro, fresh (1 bunch)
Cinnamon, ground
Cloves, ground
Coriander, ground
Cumin, ground
Dill, fresh (1 bunch)
Fennel powder
Garlic powder
Ginger, fresh (2 teaspoons)
Ginger, ground
Green chili powder

Mustard, ground
Nutmeg, ground
Oregano, dried
Oregano, fresh (1 bunch)
Paprika, sweet
Parsley, fresh (1 bunch)
Peppercorns, black
Red pepper flakes
Thyme, dried
Thyme, fresh (1 bunch)
Turmeric, ground

Fish and Seafood

Cod (4 fillets totaling 12 ounces)
Salmon (4 fillets totaling 12 ounces)

Shrimp (8 ounces)
Tuna, yellowfin (4 fillets totaling 12 ounces)

Meat and Poultry

Beef, ground, 95% lean (1 pound)
Beef, roast, chuck or rump (1½ pounds, divided into 1 pound and ½ pound)
Chicken carcass (1)

Chicken breasts, boneless, skinless (24 ounces, or family pack)
Chicken thighs, boneless, skinless (11)
Pork, top loin (4 chops totaling 12 ounces)

Other

Baking soda substitute, Ener-G (1½ teaspoons)
Beef stock (1 cup)
Breadcrumbs
Bread, Italian (2 slices)
Bread, white (8 slices)
Buckwheat, whole (2 tablespoons)

Bulgur (6 tablespoons)
Chickpeas, canned (4 ounces)
Cooking spray
Cornstarch
Couscous (2½ cups plus 6 tablespoons)
Flour, all-purpose

Honey
Jam, strawberry (¼ cup)
Linguine
Oil, canola
Oil, olive
Penne
Sugar, brown

Sugar, granulated
Tortillas, flour, 6-inch diameter (2)
Vanilla extract, pure
Vinegar, apple cider
Vinegar, balsamic
Vinegar, white

Week 1 Meal Plan

Monday:
Breakfast: Egg Fried Rice
Lunch: Appealing Green Salad
Dinner: Hearty Meatballs

Tuesday:
Breakfast: Blueberry Smoothie Bowl
Lunch: Easy Lemon Butter Salmon
Dinner: Pork Meatloaf

Wednesday:
Breakfast: Blueberry Pancake
Lunch: Authentic Shrimp Wraps
Dinner: Persian Chicken

Thursday:
Breakfast: Salmon Bagel Toast
Lunch: Healthier Pita Veggie Rolls
Dinner: Sliced Figs Salad

Friday:
Breakfast: Cottage Cheese Pancakes
Lunch: Orzo And Vegetables
Dinner: Mussels with Saffron

Saturday:
Breakfast: Italian Apple Fritters
Lunch: Winner Kabobs
Dinner: Chicken Stew

Sunday:
Breakfast: Vegetable Rice Casserole
Lunch: Vegetarian Egg Fried Rice
Dinner: Eggplant And Red Pepper Soup

Suggested Snacks:

- ✓ Cinnamon Applesauce
- ✓ Blueberry-Pineapple Smoothie
- ✓ Spicy Kale Chips
- ✓ Hard-boiled eggs
- ✓ Grapes
- ✓ Ice pops
- ✓ Rice cakes

Week 2 Meal Plan

Monday:
Breakfast: Traditional Scotch Eggs Recipe
Lunch: Green Bean Veggie Stew
Dinner: Fried Mussels with Mustard and Lemon

Tuesday:
Breakfast: Mock Pancakes
Lunch: Tempting Burgers
Dinner: Catalonian Shrimp Stew

Wednesday:
Breakfast: Muffins with Kale and Gruyère Cheese
Lunch: Authentic Shrimp Wraps
Dinner: Couscous Burgers

Thursday:
Breakfast: Asparagus Bacon Hash
Lunch: Mediterranean Burrito
Dinner: Best Creamy Broccoli Soup

Friday:
Breakfast: Berry and Chia Yogurt
Lunch: Loveable Tortillas
Dinner: Hearty Meatloaf

Saturday:
Breakfast: Eggs Creamy Melt
Lunch: Shrimp Fried Rice
Dinner: Chicken Stew

Sunday:

Breakfast: Sunny Pineapple Breakfast Smoothie
Lunch: Sweet Potato Bacon Mash
Dinner: Seafood Casserole

Suggested Snacks:

- ✓ Cooked Four-Pepper Salsa with baked pita wedges
- ✓ Apple-Chai Smoothie
- ✓ Meringue Cookies
- ✓ Tuna salad
- ✓ Apple
- ✓ Unsalted popcorn
- ✓ Watermelon

Shopping List for Week 3

Fruits and Vegetables

Apples (2)
Blueberries (8 ounces)
Cabbage, green, shredded (½ cup)
Carrots (2)
Celery stalks (3)
Corn, frozen kernels (2 cups)
Cucumbers, English (2)
Garlic (14 cloves or 10 teaspoons minced garlic and 2 cloves)

Lemons (6)
Lettuce, leaf, green (1 head)
Limes (5)
Onion, red (1)
Onions, sweet (2)
Peppers, bell, red (3)
Scallions (4)
Watercress (1 bunch)

Dairy and Dairy Alternatives

Butter, unsalted (¾ cup)
Cheese, cream, plain (10 ounces)
Eggs (24)
Milk, coconut (¼ cup)

Milk, rice, unsweetened (4 cups)
Milk, rice, vanilla (1¼ cups)
Sour cream, light (4 tablespoons)

Spices and Herbs

Basil, fresh (1 bunch)
Bay leaves, dried (2)
Cayenne pepper
Chives, fresh (1 bunch)
Cilantro, fresh (1 bunch)
Cinnamon, ground
Cumin, ground
Curry powder
Dill, fresh (1 bunch)
Garlic powder
Ginger, fresh (4-inch piece)
Ginger, ground

Green chili powder
Nutmeg, ground
Oregano, dried
Oregano, fresh (1 bunch)
Paprika, sweet
Parsley, fresh (1 bunch)
Peppercorns, black, freshly ground
Red pepper flakes
Sage, fresh (1 bunch)
Tarragon, fresh (1 bunch)
Thyme, fresh (1 bunch)

Fish and Seafood

Cod (4 fillets totaling 12 ounces)
Crab meat, queen (8 ounces)

Tuna, yellowfin (4 fillets totaling 12 ounces)

Meat and Poultry

Beef, ground, 95% lean (1 pound)
Beef, roast, chuck (½ pound)
Beef, steak, flank (¾ pound)
Beef, tenderloin (4 steaks totaling 12 ounces)

Chicken breasts, boneless, skinless (12 ounces)
Chicken thighs, boneless, skinless (11)
Pork, top loin (4 chops totaling 12 ounces)
Turkey, ground, 93% lean (5 ounces)

Other

Baking soda substitute, Ener-G (3½ teaspoons)
Breadcrumbs
Bread, pita pockets, 4-inch diameter (2)

Bread, white (8 slices)
Buckwheat, whole (2 tablespoons)
Bulgur (1 cup)

Chickpeas (4 ounces)
Chili paste (1 teaspoon)
Cooking spray
Cornstarch
Couscous (3 cups)
Flour, all-purpose
Honey
Hot pepper sauce
Jam, strawberry (¼ cup)
Oil, canola

Oil, olive
Penne
Stock, beef (1 cup)
Sugar, brown
Sugar, granulated
Tortillas, flour, 6-inch diameter (2)
Vanilla extract, pure
Vinegar, apple cider
Vinegar, white

Shopping List for Week 4

Fruits and Vegetables
Apples (2)
Carrots (2)
Celery stalks (4)
Corn, frozen kernels (2 cups)
Cucumber, English (1)
Garlic (14 cloves or 10 teaspoons minced garlic and 2 cloves)
Lemons (4)

Lettuce, Boston (1 head)
Limes (3)
Onions, sweet (4)
Peppers, red, bell (2)
Rhubarb (6 stalks)
Scallions (4)
Sprouts, bean (½ cup)

Dairy and Dairy Alternatives
Butter, unsalted (¾ cup)
Cheese, cream, plain (5 ounces)
Cheese, Parmesan, low-fat (1 ounce)
Eggs (25)

Milk, coconut (¼ cup)
Milk, rice, unsweetened (3¼ cups)
Milk, rice, vanilla (1¼ cups)
Sour cream, light (2 tablespoons)

Spices and Herbs
Basil, fresh (1 bunch)
Cayenne pepper
Chinese five-spice powder
Chives, fresh (1 bunch)
Cilantro, fresh (1 bunch)
Cinnamon, ground
Curry powder
Ginger, fresh (2-inch piece)
Green chili powder

Nutmeg, ground
Oregano, fresh (1 bunch)
Parsley, fresh (1 bunch)
Pepper, black, freshly ground
Red pepper flakes
Tarragon, fresh (1 bunch)
Thyme, fresh (1 bunch)
Vanilla bean (1)

Fish and Seafood
Crab meat, queen (8 ounces)
Salmon (4 fillets totaling 12 ounces)
Tuna, yellowfin (4 fillets totaling 12 ounces)

Meat and Poultry
Beef, roast, chuck (½ pound)
Beef, tenderloin (4 steaks totaling 12 ounces)
Chicken breasts, boneless, skinless (32 ounces, or family pack)

Chicken thighs, boneless, skinless (6)
Pork, chops, top loin (4 chops totaling 12 ounces)

Other
Baking soda substitute, Ener-G (½ teaspoon)
Breadcrumbs
Bread, Italian (1 loaf)
Bread, white (10 slices)
Buckwheat, whole (2 tablespoons)
Bulgur (6 tablespoons)

Chickpeas (4 ounces)
Cooking spray
Cornstarch
Couscous (2 cups)
Flour, all-purpose
Honey

Hot pepper sauce
Oil, olive
Penne
Spaghetti

Stock, beef (1 cup)
Sugar, granulated
Tortillas, flour, 6-inch diameter (2)
Vinegar, balsamic

Meal plans for Week 3

Monday:
Breakfast: Mexican Frittata
Lunch: Energetic Fruity Salad
Dinner: Egg and Fish Fry

Tuesday:
Breakfast: Poached Asparagus and Egg
Lunch: Green Pepper Slaw
Dinner: Persian Chicken

Wednesday:
Breakfast: Turkey Breakfast Sausage
Lunch: Authentic Shrimp Wraps
Dinner: Grilled King Prawns with Parsley Sauce

Thursday:
Breakfast: Cottage Cheese Pancakes
Lunch: Caraway Cabbage And Rice
Dinner: Healthy Sweet Potato Puree

Friday:
Breakfast: Savory Muffins with Protein
Lunch: Mediterranean Burrito
Dinner: Italian Turkey Meatloaf

Saturday:
Breakfast: Pineapple Bread
Lunch: Prosciutto Wrapped Mozzarella Balls
Dinner: Hearty Meatloaf

Sunday:
Breakfast: Puffy French Toast
Lunch: Beef Okra Soup
Dinner: Baked Flounder

Suggested Snacks:

- ✓ Cinnamon Applesauce
- ✓ Festive Berry Parfait
- ✓ Corn Bread
- ✓ Tuna salad
- ✓ Cucumber sticks
- ✓ Mixed berries
- ✓ Graham crackers

Meal plans for Week 4

Monday:
Breakfast: Texas Toast Casserole
Lunch: Stuffed Tomatoes with Cheese and Meat
Dinner: Eggplant and Red Pepper Soup

Tuesday:
Breakfast: Roasted Pepper Soup
Lunch: Delightful Pizza
Dinner: Pasta With Cheesy Meat Sauce

Wednesday:
Breakfast: Shrimp Bok Choy
Lunch: Healthier Pita Veggie Rolls
Dinner: Beef Burritos

Thursday:
Breakfast: Wholesome Pancakes
Lunch: Vegetarian Egg Fried Rice
Dinner: Apple Spice Pork Chops

Friday:
Breakfast: Fluffy American Blueberry Pancakes
Lunch: Greek Style Pita Rolls
Dinner: Tuna Salad with Avocado, Sesame and Mint

Saturday:
Breakfast: Cheddar and Spinach Muffins
Lunch: Orzo And Vegetables
Dinner: Aromatic Cuttlefish with Spinach

Sunday:
Breakfast: Broccoli and Vegetable "Rice" Delight
Lunch: Classic Chicken Soup
Dinner: Fried Wine Octopus Patties

Suggested Snacks:

- ✓ Cinnamon Applesauce
- ✓ Blueberry-Pineapple Smoothie
- ✓ Roasted Red Pepper and Chicken Crostini
- ✓ Deviled eggs
- ✓ Grapes
- ✓ Vanilla wafer cookies
- ✓ Carrot sticks

NOTE:

Before going into the recipes, keep in mind that the Nutritional Information refers to 100gr of product and the calories are expressed in kcal.

Chapter 4: Breakfast Recipes

1. Mixed Vegetable Barley

*Preparation Time: 15 minutes | **Cooking Time**: 35 minutes | **Servings**: 6*

Ingredients:

- 1 tablespoon olive oil
- 1 medium sweet onion, chopped
- 2 teaspoons minced garlic
- 2 cups fresh cauliflower florets
- 1 red bell pepper, diced
- 1 carrot, sliced
- ½ cup barley
- ½ cup white rice
- 2 cups water
- 1 tablespoon minced fresh parsley

Directions:

In a large skillet over medium-high heat, heat the olive oil.

Add the onion and garlic, and sauté until softened, about 3 minutes.

Stir in the cauliflower, bell pepper, and carrot, and sauté for 5 minutes.

Stir in the barley, rice, and water and bring to a boil.

Reduce the heat to low, cover, and simmer until the liquid is absorbed and the barley and rice are tender, about 25 minutes.

Serve topped with the parsley.

Nutrition	Calories	156	Fat	3g	Carbs	30g	Protein	4g	Sodium	11g	Phosphorus	83mg	Potassium	220mg

2. Spicy Sesame Tofu

*Preparation Time: 15 minutes | **Cooking Time**: 10 minutes | **Servings**: 6*

Ingredients:

- 1 tablespoon toasted sesame oil
- 1 tablespoon grated peeled fresh ginger
- 2 teaspoons minced garlic
- 2 red bell peppers, thinly sliced
- 1 (14-ounce) package extra-firm tofu, drained and cut into 1-inch cubes
- 2 cups quartered Bok choy
- 2 scallions, white and green parts, cut thinly on a bias
- 3 tablespoons low-sodium soy sauce
- 2 tablespoons freshly squeezed lime juice
- Pinch red pepper flakes
- 2 tablespoons chopped fresh cilantro
- 2 tablespoons toasted sesame seeds

Directions:

In a large skillet over medium-high heat, heat the sesame oil.

Add the ginger and garlic, and sauté until softened, about 3 minutes.

Stir in the bell peppers and tofu, and gently sauté for about 3 minutes.

Add the Bok choy and scallions, and sauté until the

Bok choy is wilted, about 3 minutes.

Add the soy sauce, lime juice, and red pepper flakes and toss to coat.

Serve topped with the cilantro and sesame seeds.

Nutrition	Calories	80	Fat	3g	Carbs	4g	Protein	6g	Sodium	503mg	Phosphorus	88mg	Potassium	165mg

3. Mushroom Rice Noodles

Preparation Time: 15 minutes | Cooking Time: 15 minutes | Servings: 4

Ingredients:

- 4 cups rice noodles
- 2 teaspoons toasted sesame oil
- 2 cups sliced wild mushrooms
- 2 teaspoons minced garlic
- 1 red bell pepper, sliced

- 1 yellow bell pepper, sliced
- 1 carrot, julienned
- 2 scallions, white and green parts, sliced
- 1 tablespoon low-sodium soy sauce

Directions:

Prepare the rice noodles according to the package instructions and set them aside.

In a large skillet over medium-high heat, heat the sesame oil.

Sauté the red bell pepper, yellow bell pepper, carrot, and scallions until tender, about 5 minutes.

Stir in the soy sauce and rice noodles and toss to coat. Serve.

Nutrition	Calories	165	Fat	2g	Carbs	33g	Protein	2g	Sodium	199mg	Phosphorus	69mg	Potassium	200mg

4. Egg Fried Rice

Preparation Time: 10 minutes | Cooking Time: 20 minutes | Servings: 6

Ingredients:

- 1 tablespoon olive oil
- 1 tablespoon grated peeled fresh ginger
- 1 teaspoon minced garlic
- 1 cup chopped carrots
- 1 scallion, white and green parts, chopped

- 2 tablespoons chopped fresh cilantro
- 4 cups cooked rice
- 1 tablespoon low-sodium soy sauce
- 4 eggs, beaten

Directions:

In a large skillet over medium-high heat, heat the olive oil.

Add the ginger and garlic, and sauté until softened, about 3 minutes.

Add the carrots, scallion, and cilantro, and sauté until tender, about 5 minutes.

Stir in the rice and soy sauce, and sauté until the rice is heated through, about 5 minutes.

Move the rice over to one side of the skillet and pour the eggs into the space.

Scramble the eggs, then mix them into the rice. Serve hot.

Nutrition	Calories	204	Fat	6g	Carbs	29g	Protein	8g	Sodium	223g	Phosphorus	120mg	Potassium	147mg

5. Vegetable Rice Casserole

Preparation Time: 10 minutes | Cooking Time: 50 minutes | Servings: 4

Ingredients:

- 1 teaspoon olive oil
- ½ small sweet onion, chopped
- ½ teaspoon minced garlic
- ½ cup chopped red bell pepper
- ¼ cup grated carrot

- 1 cup white basmati rice
- 2 cups water
- ¼ cup grated Parmesan cheese
- Freshly ground black pepper

Directions:

Preheat the oven to 350°F. In a medium skillet over medium-high heat, heat the olive oil.

Add the onion and garlic, and sauté until softened, about 3 minutes.

Transfer the vegetables to a 9-by-9-inch baking dish and stir in the rice and water.

Cover the dish and bake until the liquid is absorbed, 35 to 40 minutes.

Sprinkle the cheese on top and bake an additional 5 minutes to melt.

Season the casserole with pepper. Serve.

Nutrition	Calories	224	Fat	3g	Carbs	41g	Protein	6g	Sodium	105mg	Phosphorus	118mg	Potassium	176mg

6. Puffy French Toast

Preparation Time: 5 minutes | Cooking Time: 8 minutes | Servings: 4

Ingredients:

- 4 slices of white bread, cut in half diagonally
- 3 whole eggs and 1 egg white
- 1 cup of plain almond milk
- 2 tbsp of canola oil
- 1 tsp of cinnamon

Directions:

Preheat your oven to 400°F. Beat together the eggs with the almond milk.

Heat the oil in a pan. Dip each bread slice/triangle into the egg and almond milk mixture.

Fry in the pan until golden brown on each side.

Place the toasts in a baking dish and let cook in the oven for another 5 minutes.

Serve warm and drizzle with some honey, icing sugar, or cinnamon on top.

Nutrition	Calories	293	Fat	16g	Carbs	25g	Protein	9g	Sodium	211g	Phosphorus	165mg	Potassium	97mg

7. Savory Muffins with Protein

Preparation Time: 15 minutes | Cooking Time: 35 minutes | Servings: 12

Ingredients:

- 2 cups of corn flakes
- ½ cup of unfortified almond milk
- 4 large eggs
- 2 tbsp of olive oil
- 1/2 cup of almond milk
- 1 medium white onion, sliced
- 1 cup of plain Greek yogurt
- ¼ cup pecans, chopped
- 1 tbsp of mixed seasoning blend e.g. Mrs. dash

Directions:

Preheat the oven at 350°F. Heat the olive oil in the pan.

Sauté the onions with the pecans and seasoning blend for a couple of minutes. Add the rest of Ingredients and toss well.

Split the mixture into 12 small muffin cups (lightly greased) and bake for 30-35 minutes or until an inserted knife or toothpick is coming out clean.

Serve warm or keep at room temperature for a couple of days.

Nutrition	Calories	106	Fat	6g	Carbs	8g	Protein	4g	Sodium	52mg	Phosphorus	49mg	Potassium	87mg

8. Sunny Pineapple Breakfast Smoothie

Preparation Time: 1 minutes | Cooking Time: 1 minutes | Servings: 1

Ingredients:

- ½ cup of frozen pineapple chunks
- ⅔ cup almond milk
- ½ tsp of ginger powder
- 1 tbsp of agave syrup

Directions:

Blend everything in a blender until nice and smooth (around 30 seconds).

Transfer into a tall glass or mason jar. Serve and enjoy.

Nutrition	Calories	186	Fat	6g	Carbs	43g	Protein	2g	Sodium	130mg	Phosphorus	18mg	Potassium	137mg

9. Tofu and Mushroom Scramble

Preparation Time: 5 minutes | Cooking Time: 8 minutes | Servings: 2

Ingredients:

- ½ cup of sliced white mushrooms
- ⅓ cup medium firm tofu, crumbled
- 1 tbsp of chopped shallots
- ⅓ tsp turmeric
- 1 tsp of cumin
- ⅓ tsp of smoked paprika
- ½ tsp of garlic salt
- Pepper
- 3 tbsp of vegetable oil

Directions:

Heat the oil in a medium frying pan and sauté the sliced mushrooms with the shallots until softened (around 3-4 minutes) over medium to high heat.

Add the tofu pieces and toss in the spices and the garlic salt.

Toss lightly until tofu and mushrooms are nicely combined. Serve warm.

Nutrition	Calories	220	Fat	23g	Carbs	2.6g	Protein	3g	Sodium	223mg	Phosphorus	68mg	Potassium	135mg

10. Italian Apple Fritters

Preparation Time: 5 minutes | Cooking Time: 8 minutes | Servings: 4

Ingredients:

- 2 large apples, seeded, peeled and thickly sliced in circles
- 3 tbsp of corn flour
- ½ tsp of water
- 1 tsp of sugar
- 1 tsp of cinnamon
- Vegetable oil (for frying)
- Sprinkle of icing sugar or honey

Directions:

In a small bowl, combine the corn flour, water and sugar to make your batter.

Deep the apple rounds into the corn flour mix. Heat enough vegetable oil to cover half of the pan's surface over medium to high heat.

Add the apple rounds into the pan and cook until golden brown.

Transfer into a shallow dish with absorbing paper on top and sprinkle with a bit of cinnamon and icing sugar.

Nutrition	Calories	183	Fat	6g	Carbs	17g	Protein	0.3g	Sodium	2mg	Phosphorus	12mg	Potassium	100mg

11. Turkey Breakfast Sausage

Preparation Time: *3 minutes* | ***Cooking Time:*** *6 minutes* | ***Servings:*** *6*

Ingredients:

- 1 pound of lean ground turkey
- 1 tsp of fennel seed
- ¼ tsp garlic powder
- ¼ tsp onion powder
- ¼ tsp salt
- 2 tbsp of vegetable oil
- Pepper

Directions:

Combine all the ingredients apart from the vegetable oil in a mixing bowl.

Form into long and flat (around 4 inch-long) patties.

Heat the vegetable oil in a medium frying pan.

Add 3-4 patties at a time and cook for approx. 3 minutes on each side.

Repeat until you cook all patties. Serve warm.

Nutrition	Calories	74	Fat	5g	Carbs	0.1g	Protein	7g	Sodium	122mg	Phosphorus	75mg	Potassium	89mg

12. Blueberry Smoothie Bowl

Preparation Time: *1 minutes* | ***Cooking Time:*** *1 minutes* | ***Servings:*** *1*

Ingredients:

- ½ cup of frozen blueberries
- ½ cup of vanilla flavored almond milk
- 1 tbsp of agave syrup
- 1 tsp of chia seeds

Directions:

Combine everything except for the chia seeds in the blender until smooth.

You should end up with a thick smoothie paste.

Transfer into a cereal bowl and top with chia seeds on top.

Nutrition	Calories	278	Fat	6g	Carbs	39g	Protein	1.3g	Sodium	76mg	Phosphorus	59mg	Potassium	229mg

13. Egg White and Pepper Omelets

Preparation Time: *2 minutes* | ***Cooking Time:*** *5 minutes* | ***Servings:*** *1-2*

Ingredients:

- 4 egg whites, lightly beaten
- 1 red bell pepper, diced
- 1 tsp of paprika
- 2 tbsp. of olive oil
- ½ tsp of salt
- Pepper

Directions:

In a shallow pan (around 8 inches), heat the olive oil and sauté the bell peppers until softened.

Add the egg whites and the paprika and fold the edges into the fluid center with a spatula and let omelet cook until eggs are fully opaque and solid. Season with salt and pepper.

Nutrition	Calories	165	Fat	6g	Carbs	3.9g	Protein	9.3g	Sodium	767mg	Phosphorus	202mg	Potassium	193mg

14. Chicken Egg Rolls

Preparation Time: 10 minutes | Cooking Time: 12 minutes | Servings: 14

Ingredients:

- 1 lb. cooked chicken, diced
- 1/2 lb. bean sprouts
- 1/2 lb. cabbage, shredded
- 1 cup onion, chopped
- 2 tablespoons olive oil

- 1 tablespoon low sodium soy sauce
- 1 garlic clove, minced
- 20 egg roll wrappers
- Oil for frying

Directions:

Add everything to a suitable bowl except for the roll wrappers. Mix these Ingredients: well to prepare the filling then marinate for 30 minutes.

Place the roll wrappers on the working surface and divide the prepared filling on them. Fold the roll wrappers as per the package instructions and keep them aside.

Add oil to a deep wok and heat it to 350°F. Deep the egg rolls until golden brown on all sides.

Transfer the egg rolls to a plate lined with a paper towel to absorb all the excess oil. Serve warm.

Nutrition	Calories	212	Fat	3.8g	Carbs	29g	Protein	14.3g	Sodium	329mg	Phosphorus	361mg	Potassium	171mg

15. Pork Bread Casserole

Preparation Time: 20 minutes | Cooking Time: 55 minutes | Servings: 8

Ingredients:

- 2 tablespoons butter
- 1 lb. pork sausage
- 1 yellow onion, chopped
- 18 slices white bread, cut into cubes
- 2 ½ cups sharp Cheddar cheese, grated

- 1/2 cup fresh parsley, chopped
- 6 large eggs
- 2 cups half-and-half cream
- 1 teaspoon garlic powder
- 1/4 teaspoon black pepper

Directions:

Switch on your gas oven and preheat it at 325°F. Layer a 9x9 inches casserole dish with bread cubes.

Set a suitable-sized skillet over medium-high heat then crumb the sausage in it.

Cook the sausage until golden brown, then keep it aside. Blend the eggs with the remaining Ingredients: in a blender until smooth.

Stir in the sausage and spread this mixture over the bread pieces.

Bake the bread casserole for 55 minutes approximately in the preheated oven. Slice and serve.

Nutrition	Calories	366	Fat	15g	Carbs	15g	Protein	17.3g	Sodium	463mg	Phosphorus	501mg	Potassium	231mg

16. Salmon Bagel Toast

Preparation Time: 10 minutes | Cooking Time: 5 minutes | Servings: 2

Ingredients:

- 1 plain bagel, cut in half
- 2 tablespoons cream cheese
- 1/3 cup English cucumber, thinly sliced

- 3 oz. smoked salmon, sliced
- 3 rings red onion
- 1/2 teaspoon capers, drained

Directions:

Toast each half of the bagel in a skillet until golden brown.

Cover one of the toasted halves with cream cheese.

Set the cucumber, salmon, and capers on top of each bagel half.

Nutrition	Calories	233	Fat	6g	Carbs	27g	Protein	14g	Sodium	1137mg	Phosphorus	79mg	Potassium	151mg

17. Cinnamon Toast Strata

Preparation Time: 10 minutes | Cooking Time: 50 minutes | Servings: 12

Ingredients:

- 1 lb. loaf cinnamon raisin bread, cubed
- 8 oz. package cream cheese, diced
- 1 cup apples, peeled and diced
- 8 eggs
- 2 1/2 cups half-and-half cream
- 6 tablespoons butter, melted
- 1/4 cup maple syrup

Directions:

Layer a 9x13 inch baking dish with cooking spray.

Place ½ of the bread cubes in the greased baking dish.

Cover the bread cubes with cream cheese, apples, and the other half of the bread.

Beat the eggs with the melted butter and maple syrup in a bowl.

Pour this egg-butter mixture over the bread layer then refrigerate for 2 hours.

Bake this bread-egg casserole for 50 minutes at 325°F.

Slice and garnish with pancake syrup.

Nutrition	Calories	278	Fat	21g	Carbs	14g	Protein	7.3g	Sodium	206mg	Phosphorus	263mg	Potassium	162mg

18. Cottage Cheese Pancakes

Preparation Time: 10 minutes | Cooking Time: 10 minutes | Servings: 4

Ingredients:

- 1 cup cottage cheese
- 1/3 cup all-purpose flour
- 2 tablespoons vegetable oil
- 3 eggs, lightly beaten

Directions:

Begin by beating the eggs in a suitable bowl then stir in the cottage cheese.

Once it is well mixed, stir in the flour.

Pour a teaspoon of vegetable oil in a non-stick skillet and heat it.

Add ¼ cup of the batter in the skillet and cook for 2 minutes per side until brown.

Cook more of the pancakes using the remaining batter. Serve.

Nutrition	Calories	196	Fat	11.3g	Carbs	10.3g	Protein	13g	Sodium	276mg	Phosphorus	187mg	Potassium	110mg

19. Asparagus Bacon Hash

Preparation Time: 10 minutes | Cooking Time: 27 minutes | Servings: 4

Ingredients:

- 6 slices bacon, diced
- 1/2 onion, chopped
- 2 cloves garlic, sliced
- 2 lb. asparagus, trimmed and chopped
- Black pepper, to taste
- 2 tablespoons Parmesan, grated
- 4 large eggs
- 1/4 teaspoon red pepper flakes

Directions:

Add the asparagus and a tablespoon of water to a microwave-proof bowl.

Cover the veggies and microwave them for 5 minutes until tender.

Set a suitable non-stick skillet over moderate heat and layer it with cooking spray.

Stir in the onion and sauté for 7 minutes, then toss in the garlic.

Stir for 1 minute, then toss in the asparagus, eggs, and red pepper flakes.

Reduce the heat to low and cover the vegetables in the pan.

Top the eggs with Parmesan cheese.

Cook for approximately 15 minutes, then slice to serve.

Nutrition	Calories	290	Fat	16g	Carbs	11.6g	Protein	23.3g	Sodium	265mg	Phosphorus	247mg	Potassium	715mg

20. Cheese Spaghetti Frittata

Preparation Time: 10 minutes | Cooking Time: 10 minutes | Servings: 6

Ingredients:

- 4 cups whole-wheat spaghetti, cooked
- 4 teaspoons olive oil
- 3 medium onions, chopped
- 4 large eggs
- ½ cup milk
- ⅓ cup Parmesan cheese, grated
- 2 tablespoons fresh parsley, chopped
- 2 tablespoons fresh basil, chopped
- ½ teaspoon black pepper
- 1 tomato, diced

Directions:

Set a suitable non-stick skillet over moderate heat and add in the olive oil.

Place the spaghetti in the skillet and cook by stirring for 2 minutes on moderate heat.

Whisk the eggs with milk, parsley, and black pepper in a bowl.

Pour this milky egg mixture over the spaghetti and top it all with basil, cheese, and tomato.

Cover the spaghetti frittata again with a lid and cook for approximately 8 minutes on low heat.

Slice and serve.

Nutrition	Calories	230	Fat	7.8g	Carbs	32g	Protein	11.2g	Sodium	76mg	Phosphorus	368mg	Potassium	214mg

21. Pineapple Bread

Preparation Time: 20 minutes | *Cooking Time:* 1 hour | *Servings:* 10

Ingredients:

- 1/3 cup Swerve
- 1/3 cup butter, unsalted
- 2 eggs
- 2 cups flour

- 3 teaspoons baking powder
- 1 cup pineapple, undrained
- 6 cherries, chopped

Directions:

Whisk the Swerve with the butter in a mixer until fluffy.

Stir in the eggs, then beat again.

Add the baking powder and flour, then mix well until smooth.

Fold in the cherries and pineapple.

Spread this cherry-pineapple batter in a 9x5 inch baking pan.

Bake the pineapple batter for 1 hour at 350 °F. Slice the bread and serve.

Nutrition	Calories	197	Fat	7.2g	Carbs	18.3g	Protein	4.3g	Sodium	85mg	Phosphorus	316mg	Potassium	227mg

22. Parmesan Zucchini Frittata

Preparation Time: 10 minutes | *Cooking Time:* 35 minutes | *Servings:* 6

Ingredients:

- 1 tablespoon olive oil
- 1 cup yellow onion, sliced
- 3 cups zucchini, chopped
- ½ cup Parmesan cheese, grated

- 8 large eggs
- ½ teaspoon black pepper
- ⅛ teaspoon paprika
- 3 tablespoons parsley, chopped

Directions:

Toss the zucchinis with the onion, parsley, and all other Ingredients: in a large bowl.

Pour this zucchini-garlic mixture in an 11x7 inches pan and spread it evenly.

Bake the zucchini casserole for approximately 35 minutes at 350°F.

Cut in slices and serve.

Nutrition	Calories	142	Fat	9.7g	Carbs	4.7g	Protein	10.3g	Sodium	123mg	Phosphorus	375mg	Potassium	289mg

23. Texas Toast Casserole

Preparation Time: 10 minutes | *Cooking Time:* 30 minutes | *Servings:* 10

Ingredients:

- 1/2 cup butter, melted
- 1 cup brown Swerve
- 1 lb. Texas Toast bread, sliced
- 4 large eggs
- Maple syrup for serving

- 1 1/2 cup milk
- 1 tablespoon vanilla extract
- 2 tablespoons Swerve
- 2 teaspoons cinnamon

Directions:

Layer a 9x13 inches baking pan with cooking spray. Spread the bread slices at the bottom of the prepared pan.

Whisk the eggs with the remaining Ingredients: in a mixer.

Pour this mixture over the bread slices evenly. Bake the bread for 30 minutes at 350°F in a preheated oven and serve.

Nutrition	Calories	332	Fat	13.7g	Carbs	22.6g	Protein	7.4g	Sodium	350mg	Phosphorus	189mg	Potassium	74mg

24. Garlic Mayo Bread

***Preparation Time:** 10 minutes* | ***Cooking Time:** 5 minutes* | ***Servings:** 16*

Ingredients:

- 3 tablespoons vegetable oil
- 4 cloves garlic, minced
- 2 teaspoons paprika
- Dash cayenne pepper
- 1 teaspoon lemon juice
- 2 tablespoons Parmesan cheese, grated
- 3/4 cup mayonnaise
- 1 loaf (1 lb.) French bread, sliced
- 1 teaspoon Italian herbs

Directions:

Mix the garlic with the oil in a small bowl and leave it overnight.

Discard the garlic from the bowl and keep the garlic-infused oil. Mix the garlic-oil with cayenne, paprika, lemon juice, mayonnaise, and Parmesan.

Place the bread slices in a baking tray lined with parchment paper. Top these slices with the mayonnaise mixture and drizzle the Italian herbs on top.

Broil these slices for 5 minutes until golden brown. Serve warm.

Nutrition	Calories	217	Fat	7.9g	Carbs	30g	Protein	7g	Sodium	423mg	Phosphorus	374mg	Potassium	72mg

25. Strawberry Topped Waffles

***Preparation Time:** 15 minutes* | ***Cooking Time:** 20 minutes* | ***Servings:** 5*

Ingredients:

- 1 cup flour
- 1/4 cup Swerve
- 1 ¾ teaspoons baking powder
- 1 egg, separated
- ¾ cup milk
- ½ cup butter, melted
- ½ teaspoon vanilla extract
- Fresh strawberries, sliced

Directions:

Prepare and preheat your waffle pan following the instructions of the machine.

Begin by mixing the flour with Swerve and baking soda in a bowl. Separate the egg yolks from the egg whites, keeping them in two separate bowls. Add the milk and vanilla extract to the egg yolks. Stir the melted butter and mix well until smooth. Now beat the egg whites with an electric beater until foamy and fluffy.

Fold this fluffy composition in the egg yolk mixture.

Mix it gently until smooth, then add in the flour mixture. Stir again to make a smooth mixture.

Pour a half cup of the waffle batter in a preheated pan and cook until the waffle is done. Cook more waffles with the remaining batter. Serve fresh with strawberries on top.

Nutrition	Calories	342	Fat	20g	Carbs	21g	Protein	4.3g	Sodium	156mg	Phosphorus	126mg	Potassium	233mg

26. Simple Fluffy Sour Cream Pancakes

Preparation Time: *15 minutes* | ***Cooking Time:*** *20 minutes* | ***Servings:*** *4*

Ingredients:

- 1 cup milk
- 1/2 cup sour cream
- 1 egg, slightly beaten
- 2 tablespoons sugar
- 2 tablespoons butter, melted
- 1 teaspoon vanilla extract
- 1 & 1/2 cup all-purpose flour
- 2 teaspoons baking powder
- 1 teaspoon baking soda
- 1/4 teaspoon salt

Directions:

These simple and fluffy sour cream pancakes are delicious! They are easy to make and require little effort.

The secret to a fluffy pancake is to let the batter sit for about 15 minutes on the counter-top or overnight in the fridge.

Whisk together the egg, sugar, milk, sour cream, butter, and vanilla extract. Combine the flour, baking powder, baking soda, and salt in a separate bowl

Add the flour mixture to the liquid mixture and whisk together until no large clumps remain. Let the batter sit for 15 minutes. You can even refrigerate it overnight and cook the next morning Heat a nonstick pan on medium/low heat. Spray with oil or melt a dab of butter in the pan. Add the butter and cook for about 2 minutes on each side.

Serve immediately. Garnish with fresh fruit or just a simple drizzle of sticky maple syrup! Feel free to customize the recipe and add fresh fruit or nuts into the batter; I can picture how delicious it will taste with the addition of blueberries!

Nutrition	Calories	125	Fat	6g	Carbs	29g	Protein	15g	Sodium	48mg	Phosphorus	159mg	Potassium	279mg

27. Healthy Apple Muesli

Preparation Time: *10 minutes* | ***Cooking Time:*** *0 minutes* | ***Servings:*** *1*

Ingredients:

- 1/2 cup raw quick oats
- 1 cup milk (any type, unsweetened)
- 1 tbsp. chia seeds (or flax)
- 1/4 cup grated apple
- 1/4 tsp. ground cinnamon
- Maple syrup to taste

Directions:

A nutrition-dense breakfast that will keep you full until lunch! Combine all ingredients in a bowl and serve.

Nutrition	Calories	375	Fat	14g	Carbs	49g	Protein	13g	Sodium	108mg	Phosphorus	159mg	Potassium	297mg

28. Mexican Frittata

Preparation Time: *15 minutes* | ***Cooking Time:*** *20 minutes* | ***Servings:*** *4*

Ingredients:

- ½ cup almond milk
- 5 large eggs
- ¼ cup onions, chopped
- ¼ cup green bell pepper, chopped

Directions:

Preheat the oven to 400° F. Using a large bowl, combine almond milk, eggs, onion, and green bell pepper. Whisk until all ingredients are well combined. Transfer the mixture to a baking dish. Bake for 20 minutes. Serve.

Nutrition	Calories	385	Fat	12g	Carbs	39g	Protein	16.3g	Sodium	216mg	Phosphorus	59mg	Potassium	243mg

29. Olive Oil and Sesame Asparagus

Preparation Time: 15 minutes | *Cooking Time: 20 minutes* | *Servings: 4*

Ingredients:

- ½ cup of water
- 2 cups asparagus, sliced
- ½ tablespoon olive oil, add more for drizzling
- 1/8 teaspoon red pepper flakes, crushed
- ½ teaspoon sesame seeds

Directions:

In a large skillet, bring water to a boil.

Add in asparagus. Allow to boil for 2 minutes.

Reduce the heat and cook for another 5 minutes.

Drain asparagus and place on a plate. Set aside.

Meanwhile, heat the olive oil. Tip in asparagus and red pepper flakes. Sauté for 3 minutes.

Remove from heat. Drizzle in more olive oil and sprinkle sesame seeds before serving.

Nutrition	Calories	415	Fat	7g	Carbs	39g	Protein	6.3g	Sodium	9mg	Phosphorus	59mg	Potassium	547mg

30. Roasted Pepper Soup

Preparation Time: 15 minutes | *Cooking Time: 30 minutes* | *Servings: 4*

Ingredients:

- 2 tablespoons olive oil
- 2 large red peppers
- ½ cup onion, chopped
- 2 garlic cloves, minced
- ½ cup carrots, chopped
- ½ cup celery, chopped
- 2 cups vegetable broth, unsalted
- ½ cup almond milk
- ¼ cup sweet basil, julienned

Directions:

Place the oven into the 375°F.

Put onions on a baking sheet. Add the red peppers beside the mixture. Drizzle some of the olive oil over everything and toss well to coat.

Roast for 20 minutes, or until peppers are tender and skins are wilted.

Chop the roasted red peppers and set aside. Place a pot over medium-high flame and heat through. Once hot, add the olive oil and swirl to coat.

Place the carrot, celery, and garlic into the pot and sauté until carrot and celery are tender. Add the chopped roasted red peppers. Mix well.

Pour in the vegetable broth and almond milk. Increase to high flame and bring to a boil.

Once boiling, reduce to a simmer. Simmer, uncovered, for 10 minutes. Turn off the heat and allow to cool slightly.

If desired, blend the soup using an immersion blender until the soup has reached a desired level of smoothness.

Reheat over medium flame.

Add the basil and stir to combine. Serve.

Nutrition	Calories	345	Fat	4g	Carbs	9g	Protein	1.5g	Sodium	45mg	Phosphorus	117mg	Potassium	249mg

31. Poached Asparagus and Egg

Preparation Time: *5 minutes* | ***Cooking Time:*** *20 minutes* | ***Servings:*** *4*

Ingredients:

- 1 large egg
- 4 spears asparagus
- Water, for boiling

Directions:

Half-fill a deep saucepan with water set over high heat. Let the water come to a rolling boil.

Dunk asparagus spears in water. Cook until they turn a shade brighter, about 3 minutes.

Remove from saucepan and drain on paper towels. Keep warm. Lightly season prior to serving. Slice the top off.

The egg should still be fluid inside. To serve: place asparagus spears on a small plate and serve egg on the side. Dip asparagus into egg and eat while warm.

Nutrition	Calories	245	Fat	12g	Carbs	21g	Protein	7.3g	Sodium	71mg	Phosphorus	M59g	Potassium	209mg

32. Blueberry Pancake

Preparation Time: *10 minutes* | ***Cooking Time:*** *20 minutes* | ***Servings:*** *6*

Ingredients:

- 2 tsp baking powder
- 1½ cups plain all-purpose flour
- 1 cup buttermilk
- 3 tbsp sugar
- 2 eggs, slightly beaten
- 2 tbsp no-salt margarine, melted
- 1 cup canned blueberries, rinsed or 1 cup frozen, rinsed

Directions:

Sift together sugar, baking powder, and flour into a mixing bowl.

Make a well in the center, then add remaining ingredients.

Mix into a smooth batter. Heat a heavy skillet or griddle, and grease it lightly.

Spooning out pancakes and cook until bottom is done. Flip and finish cooking.

Nutrition	Calories	223	Fat	32g	Carbs	7g	Protein	7.3g	Sodium	91mg	Phosphorus	29mg	Potassium	109mg

33. Eggs Creamy Melt

Preparation Time: *10 minutes* | ***Cooking Time:*** *20 minutes* | ***Servings:*** *6*

Ingredients:

- 2 eggs, beaten
- Italian seasoning
- 1 cup tofu, shredded
- 1 tablespoon olive oil

Directions:

In a small bowl, combine beaten eggs and Italian seasoning. Sprinkle tofu on top.

Heat the olive oil in a pan. Add the egg mixture. Cook for 4 minutes on both sides. Serve.

Nutrition	Calories	217	Fat	12g	Carbs	21g	Protein	15g	Sodium	107mg	Phosphorus	37	Potassium	216mg

34. Buttery Savoy Cabbage

Preparation Time: 10minutes | Cooking Time: 10 minutes | Servings: 6

Ingredients:

- 1/2 stick melted butter
- 1 minced garlic clove
- 1 bunch chopped scallions
- 1 pound cored and shredded Savoy cabbage, without outer leaves
- 1/2 teaspoon sea salt

- 1/2 teaspoon freshly cracked mixed peppercorn
- 1/4 teaspoon fresh grated ginger
- 1 tablespoon dry white wine
- 1/4 cup chicken stock
- 1/3 teaspoon mustard seeds
- A pinch of nutmeg

Directions:

Put a pan on a moderate flame and melt the butter.

Sauté the garlic and scallions until soft and aromatic.

Mix in the cabbage and ginger.

Cook for 10 minutes, stirring every now and then.

Add the salt, pepper, wine, chicken stock, mustard seeds and nutmeg and cook for another 5 minutes.

Check to see that the Savoy cabbage has cooked to your liking.

Nutrition	Calories	142	Fat	11.3g	Carbs	5.7g	Protein	2g	Sodium	71mg	Phosphorus	93mg	Potassium	289mg

35. Broccoli and Vegetable "Rice" Delight

Preparation Time: 10 minutes | Cooking Time: 20 minutes | Servings: 6

Ingredients:

- 1 head broccoli florets
- 1/2 stick butter
- 1 minced garlic clove
- 1/2 chopped yellow onion

- 1/2 chopped celery stalk
- 1 chopped red pepper
- 1 Aji Fantasy minced chili pepper
- Salt and ground black pepper, to taste

Directions:

Put the broccoli in your food processor and blitz. Stop when it reaches a rice-like texture.

On medium heat, melt the butter in a pan. Cook the onion for 2 – 3 minutes and then add the garlic.

Cook until it is aromatic and slightly browned.

Add the celery, the red pepper and the Aji Fantasy chill pepper and cook for 4 minutes when they should all be tender.

Mix in the broccoli "rice" and season to taste with pepper and salt.

Cook for another 5 minutes stirring every now and then.

Serve warm and if you want it as a main meal with a curry.

Serve warm and enjoy!

Nutrition	Calories	126	Fat	11g	Carbs	5.4g	Protein	1.3g	Sodium	71mg	Phosphorus	27mg	Potassium	207mg

36. Shrimp Bok Choy

Preparation Time: 10 minutes | Cooking Time: 30 minutes | Servings: 6

Ingredients:

- 2 tablespoons coconut oil
- 2 crushed garlic cloves
- 1 1/2-inch piece of freshly grated ginger
- 1/2 pound trimmed and thinly sliced Bok Choy
- 1 teaspoon cayenne pepper
- 1 tablespoon oyster sauce
- Ground black pepper and salt to taste
- 10 ounces peeled and deveined shrimp

Directions:

Put a pan on medium heat and warm up the coconut oil. Cook the garlic until it is slightly brown.

Mix in the ginger and the Bok Choy.

Then put in the cayenne pepper, oyster sauce, pepper and salt. Stir while cooking for another 5 minutes.

Put on a serving plate.

Heat the other tablespoon of coconut oil in the pan and cook the shrimp, while stirring every now and then.

It should take around 3 minutes for the shrimp to turn pink and opaque.

Put the shrimp on top of the Bok Choy and serve with lemon wedges.

Nutrition	Calories	171	Fat	8.4g	Carbs	5.8g	Protein	17g	Sodium	2.7mg	Phosphorus	120mg	Potassium	209mg

37. Cheesy Cauliflower and Mushroom Casserole

Preparation Time: 10 minutes | Cooking Time: 30 minutes | Servings: 6

Ingredients:

- 2 tablespoons lard
- 1 teaspoon yellow mustard
- 1 tablespoon Piri Piri sauce
- 1 cup aged goat cheese
- 1 cup chicken stock
- 4 lightly beaten eggs
- 1/2 Cup of sour cream
- Cup chive & onion cream cheese
- 1/2 pound thinly sliced brown Cremini mushrooms
- 1 teaspoon fresh or dry rosemary, minced
- 1/3 teaspoon freshly ground pepper
- 1/2teaspoon salt
- 1 large head cauliflower florets

Directions:

Preheat the oven to 300°F. Spray a casserole dish with nonstick cooking spray.

Preheat a pan over medium heat and then melt the lard.

Put in the mustard, Piri Piri sauce, goat cheese, cream cheese, sour cream, chicken stock and eggs.

Cook these until they're hot.

In the baking dish layer, the cauliflower with the mushrooms.

Season with pepper, salt and rosemary.

Put the other mixture on top of the vegetables and cook for 25 – 30 minutes. Best served hot.

Nutritio	Calorie	27	Fa	21	Carb	5.3	Protei	14	Sodiu	31m	Phosphor	47m	Potassiu	109m

38. Mushroom Tofu Breakfast

Preparation Time: 10 minutes | Cooking Time: 10 minutes | Servings: 2

Ingredients:

- 1 tablespoon of chopped shallots
- ½ cup of sliced white mushrooms
- ⅓ cup medium-firm tofu, crumbled
- ⅓ teaspoon turmeric
- 1 teaspoon of cumin

- ⅓ teaspoon of smoked paprika
- 3 tablespoons of vegetable oil
- Pinch garlic salt
- Pepper

Directions:

Take a medium saucepan or skillet, add oil. Heat over medium heat.

Add shallots, mushrooms, and stir-cook until they become softened for 3-4 minutes.

Add tofu, salt, spices, and stir-cook until tofu is tender and cooked well. Serve warm.

Nutrition	Calories	217	Fat	21g	Carbs	3g	Protein	4g	Sodium	301mg	Phosphorus	77mg	Potassium	147mg

39. Cheddar and Spinach Muffins

Preparation Time: 10 minutes | Cooking Time: 20 minutes | Servings: 6

Ingredients:

- 8 eggs
- 1 cup full-fat milk
- 2 tablespoons olive oil
- 1/4 teaspoon ground black pepper

- 1/3 teaspoon salt
- 1 cup chopped spinach
- 1 ½ cups grated cheddar cheese

Directions:

Put your oven on to 350°F. Mix together the oil, eggs and milk. Add the pepper and salt, the spinach and the cheese.

Combine well. Put the mixture into a greased muffin tin. Put in the oven and bake for 25 minutes. The muffins should spring back when touched.

Nutrition	Calories	252	Fat	19g	Carbs	2g	Protein	16g	Sodium	71mg	Phosphorus	49mg	Potassium	71mg

40. Muffins with Kale and Gruyère Cheese

Preparation Time: 10 minutes | Cooking Time: 30 minutes | Servings: 6

Ingredients:

- 1/2 cup full-fat milk
- 1/2 teaspoon dried basil
- 1 1/2 cup grated Gruyere cheese
- Sea salt to taste

- 5 eggs
- 1/2 pound chopped prosciutto
- 10 ounces cooked and drained kale

Directions:

Preheat your oven to 360°F. Spray a muffin tin with a nonstick cooking spray.

Whisk together the eggs, milk, basil, Gruyere cheese and salt. Then put in the prosciutto and the kale.

Put the mixture in the muffin tin, making sure that each muffin cup is filled 3/4 full. Bake for around 25 minutes. They are good served with sour cream.

Nutrition	Calories	275	Fat	12g	Carbs	2.1g	Protein	21.3g	Sodium	174mg	Phosphorus	123mg	Potassium	114mg

41. Mock Pancakes

Preparation Time: *10 minutes* | **Cooking Time:** *20 minutes* | **Servings:** *6*

Ingredients:

- 1 egg
- 1 cup ricotta cheese
- 1 teaspoon cinnamon
- 2 tablespoons honey, add more if needed

Directions:

Using a blender, put together egg, honey, cinnamon, and ricotta cheese. Process until all ingredients are well combined.

Pour an equal amount of the blended mixture into the pan.

Cook each pancake for 4 minutes on both sides. Serve.

Nutrition	Calories	315	Fat	12g	Carbs	21g	Protein	17g	Sodium	136mg	Phosphorus	59mg	Potassium	177mg

42. Family Vegetable Pizza

Preparation Time: *10 minutes* | **Cooking Time:** *30 minutes* | **Servings:** *6*

Ingredients:

- For the Crust:
- A spray coating
- 1-pound cauliflower
- 1 tablespoon olive oil
- 1/2 cup Edam cheese
- 1/4 cup heavy cream
- 4 medium-sized eggs
- Salt, to taste
- For the Topping:
- 1 cup spring mix
- 2 tablespoons finely chopped chives
- 1 tablespoon fresh sage
- 3/4 cup sugar-free tomato sauce
- 1/4 cup pitted and sliced Kalamata olives
- 1 cup mozzarella cheese

Directions:

Cut the cauliflower into florets and cook in a large pot of salted water until soft. Add the basil-infused oil, Edam cheese, heavy cream, 4 eggs and salt.

Preheat your oven to 380°F. Grease a baking tin with nonstick spray.

Put the crust mixture in the baking tin and bake for 15 minutes in the middle of the oven.

Take out of the oven and put on the spring mix, the chives, sage, tomato sauce and the olives. End up sprinkling the mozzarella cheese on top of the pizza.

Put back in the oven until the cheese has melted.

Add some grinds of black pepper if desired or parmesan cheese.

Nutrition	Calories	235	Fat	12g	Carbs	13g	Protein	16.3g	Sodium	101mg	Phosphorus	79mg	Potassium	219mg

43. Herbed Omelet

Preparation Time: *5 minutes* | **Cooking Time:** *8-10 minutes* | **Servings:** *2*

Ingredients:

- 4 eggs
- 2 tablespoons water
- 1 ½ teaspoons vegetable oil
- 1 tablespoon chopped onion
- ¼ teaspoon basil
- ⅛ teaspoon tarragon
- ¼ teaspoon parsley (optional)

Directions:

Take a mixing bowl and beat eggs. Add water and spices and combine.

Take a medium saucepan or skillet, add oil. Heat over medium heat.

Add onion and stir-cook until become translucent and softened. Set aside.

Add the egg mixture in the pan and spread evenly.

Cook over both sides until well set and lightly brown.

Serve warm with cooked onions on top.

Nutrition	Calories	204	Fat	14g	Carbs	1g	Protein	14g	Sodium	174mg	Phosphorus	201mg	Potassium	166mg

44. Wholesome Pancakes

Preparation Time: 10 minutes | Cooking Time: 20 minutes | Servings: 2

Ingredients:

- ¼ teaspoon ground cinnamon
- Pinch ground nutmeg
- 2 eggs
- ½ cup unsweetened almond or rice milk
- ½ cup all-purpose flour

Directions:

Preheat an oven to 450⁰F. In a mixing bowl, add milk and eggs.

Whisk to mix well with each other.

Add flour, cinnamon, and nutmeg; combine to blend well.

Take an oven-proof skillet; grease with some cooking spray.

Spreads batter over it evenly and bake for about 20 minutes until you see crisp edges and puffed up.

Slice in halves and serve warm.

Nutrition	Calories	173	Fat	1g	Carbs	28g	Protein	7.3g	Sodium	51mg	Phosphorus	85mg	Potassium	122mg

45. Healthy Mushroom Frittata

Preparation Time: 5 minutes | Cooking Time: 20 minutes | Servings: 4

Ingredients:

- 1 tablespoon olive oil
- 16 oz button mushrooms, sliced
- 8 large eggs
- 1/4 cup plain Greek yogurt or sour cream
- 1/4 teaspoon sea salt
- 1/4 teaspoon black pepper
- 1/4 teaspoon dried thyme
- 1/2 cup chopped scallions, green parts
- 1/2 cup grated Parmesan cheese
- Olive oil spray

Directions:

Preheat oven to 400 °F. Place a 9-inch pie dish in the oven to warm it up.

Heat the olive oil in a large skillet over medium heat.

Add the mushrooms. Cook the mushrooms until browned and tender and all liquids have evaporated, about 10 minutes.

Beat the eggs with the yogurt, salt, pepper and thyme. Add the scallions and the cheese, mixing them in with a spatula.

Remove the warm pie dish from the oven using oven mitts and spray it with olive oil spray (or brush with olive oil).

46

Transfer the mushrooms to the baking dish. Pour the egg mixture on top.

Return the baking dish to the oven and bake until edges are brown, frittata is golden brown and puffy, and a knife inserted in center comes out clean, about 30 minutes.

Allow to cool 10 minutes, then slice into eight triangles and serve.

Nutrition	Calories	245	Fat	12g	Carbs	6g	Protein	23.3g	Sodium	561mg	Phosphorus	59mg	Potassium	209mg

46. Berry and Chia Yogurt

Preparation Time: 10 minutes | Cooking Time: 0 minutes | Servings: 4

Ingredients:

- 2 cups plain Greek yogurt
- 2 teaspoons chia seeds
- 2 tablespoons honey
- 1/4 teaspoon cinnamon
- 1/2 cup Clean granola, we used KIND
- 1/2 cup fresh berries (any kind will work)

Directions:

Combine yogurt, chia seeds, honey, and cinnamon, Whisk to combine.

If desired, sprinkle a few slivered almonds on top.

Serve and enjoy!

Nutrition	Calories	252	Fat	12g	Carbs	25g	Protein	13g	Sodium	72mg	Phosphorus	79mg	Potassium	187mg

47. Fluffy American Blueberry Pancakes

Preparation Time: 15 minutes | Cooking Time: 20 minutes | Servings: 10

Ingredients:

- 200g self-rising flour
- 1 tsp baking powder
- 1 egg
- 300ml milk
- Golden or maple syrup

Directions:

Mix together 200g self-rising flour, 1 tsp baking powder and a pinch of salt in a large bowl.

Beat 1 egg with 300ml milk, make a well in the center of the dry ingredients and whisk in the milk to make a thick smooth batter.

Beat in a knob of melted butter, and gently stir in half of the 150g pack of blueberries.

Heat a teaspoon of sunflower oil or small knob of butter in a large nonstick frying pan.

Drop a large tablespoonful of the batter per pancake into the pan to make pancakes about 7.5cm across.

Make three or four pancakes at a time.

Cook for about 3 minutes over a medium heat until small bubbles appear on the surface of each pancake, then turn and cook another 2-3 minutes until golden.

Cover with kitchen paper to keep warm while you use up the rest of the batter.

Serve with golden or maple syrup and the rest of the blueberries.

Nutritio	Calorie	108	Fat	3g	Carb	18g	Protei	4.6	Sodiu	41m	Phosphoru	69m	Potassiu	81m

48. Traditional Scotch Eggs Recipe

Preparation Time: 20 minutes | Cooking Time: 20 minutes | Servings: 5

Ingredients:

- ½ teaspoon paprika powder
- 1 ½ pounds ground pork
- 1 egg, beaten

- 1 garlic clove minced
- 5 eggs, hardboiled and peeled

Directions:

Combine the beaten egg, ground pork, garlic, and paprika in a mixing bowl. Season with salt and pepper to taste. Divide the meat mixture into 5 balls.

Flatten the balls with your hands and place an egg at the center. Cover the egg with the meat mixture. Do the same thing with the other balls.

Place a nonstick pan on medium fire and cook ground pork coating for 4 minutes per side. Serve and enjoy.

Nutrition	Calories	481	Fat	32g	Carbs	0.7g	Protein	42g	Sodium	175mg	Phosphorus	59mg	Potassium	573mg

Chapter 5: Lunch Recipes

49. Energetic Fruity Salad

*Preparation Time: 20 minutes | **Cooking Time**: 15 minutes | **Servings**: 12*

Ingredients:

- For Dressing:
- ½ cup of fresh pineapple juice
- 2 tbsp. of fresh lemon juice
- For Salad:
- 2 cups of hulled and sliced fresh strawberries

- 2 cups of fresh blackberries
- 2 cups of fresh blueberries
- 1 cup of halved seedless red grapes
- 1 cup of halved seedless red grapes
- 6 cored and chopped fresh apples

Directions:

In a bowl, add all dressing ingredients and beat until well combined. Keep aside.

In another large bowl, mix all salad ingredients.

Add dressing and gently, toss to coat well.

Refrigerate, covered to chill before serving.

Nutrition	Calories	116	Fat	0.5g	Carbs	29g	Protein	1.2g	Sodium	3mg	Phosphorus	49mg	Potassium	276mg

50. Appealing Green Salad

*Preparation Time: 50 minutes | **Cooking Time**: 15 minutes | **Servings**: 4*

Ingredients:

- For Dressing:
- 1 tbsp. of shallot, minced
- 1/3 cup of olive oil
- 2 tbsp. of fresh lemon juice
- 1 tsp. of honey

- Freshly ground black pepper, to taste
- For Salad:
- 1½ cups of chopped broccoli florets
- 1½ cups of shredded cabbage
- 4 cups of chopped lettuce

Directions:

In a bowl, add all dressing ingredients and beat until well combined. Keep aside.

In another large bowl, mix all salad ingredients

Add dressing and gently, toss to coat well.

Serve immediately.

Nutrition	Calories	179	Fat	17g	Carbs	7.5g	Protein	1.7g	Sodium	21mg	Phosphorus	99mg	Potassium	249mg

51. Excellent Veggie Sandwiches

*Preparation Time: 30 minutes | **Cooking Time**: 15 minutes | **Servings**: 8*

Ingredients:

- 1 sliced large tomato
- ½ of sliced cucumber
- ½ cup of thinly sliced red onion

- 1 cup of chopped romaine lettuce leaves
- ½ cup of low-sodium mayonnaise
- 8 toasted white bread slices

49

Directions:

In a large bowl, mix together tomato, cucumber, onion and lettuce.

Spread mayonnaise over each slice evenly. Divide tomato mixture over 4 slices evenly.

Cover with remaining slices. With a knife, carefully cut the sandwiches diagonally and serve.

Nutrition	Calories	92	Fat	5.3g	Carbs	10g	Protein	1.2g	Sodium	168mg	Phosphorus	109mg	Potassium	168mg

52. Lunchtime Staple Sandwiches
Preparation Time: 40 minutes | Cooking Time: 15 minutes | Servings: 2

Ingredients:

- 3 tsp. of low-sodium mayonnaise
- 2 toasted white bread slices
- 3 tbsp. of chopped unsalted cooked turkey
- 2 thin apple slices
- 2 tbsp. of low-fat cheddar cheese
- 1 tsp. of olive oil

Directions:

Spread mayonnaise over each slice evenly. Place turkey over 1 slice, followed by apple slices and cheese.

Cover with remaining slice to make sandwich.

Grease a large nonstick frying pan with oil and heat on medium heat.

Place the sandwich in frying pan and with the back of spoon, gently, press down.

Cook for about 1-2 minutes.

Carefully, flip the whole sandwich and cook for about 1-2 minutes.

Transfer the sandwich into serving plate. With a knife, carefully cut the sandwich diagonally ad serve.

Nutrition	Calories	239	Fat	8.5g	Carbs	37g	Protein	7.3g	Sodium	169mg	Phosphorus	59mg	Potassium	171mg

53. Greek Style Pita Rolls
Preparation Time: 20 minutes | Cooking Time: 20 minutes | Servings: 5

Ingredients:

- 2 (6½-inch) pita breads
- 1 tbsp. of low-fat cream cheese
- 1 peeled, cored and thinly sliced apple
- Olive oil cooking spray, as required
- 1/8 tsp. of ground cinnamon

Directions:

Preheat the oven to 400°F.

In a microwave safe plate, place tortillas and microwave for about 10 seconds to soften.

Spread the cream cheese over each tortilla evenly.

Arrange apple slices in the center of each tortilla evenly.

Roll tortillas to secure the filling.

Arrange the tortilla rolls onto a baking sheet in a single layer.

Spray the rolls with cooking spray evenly and sprinkle with cinnamon. Bake for about 10 minutes or until top becomes golden brown.

Nutrition	Calories	129	Fat	2.2g	Carbs	24g	Protein	3.3g	Sodium	167mg	Phosphorus	101mg	Potassium	102mg

54. Healthier Pita Veggie Rolls

Preparation Time: 30 minutes | Cooking Time: 15 minutes | Servings: 6

Ingredients:

- 1 cup of shredded romaine lettuce
- 1 seeded and chopped red bell pepper
- ½ cup of chopped cucumber
- 1 small seeded and chopped tomato
- 1 small chopped red onion

- 1 finely minced garlic clove
- 1 tbsp. of olive oil
- ½ tbsp. of fresh lemon juice
- Freshly ground black pepper, to taste
- 3 (6½-inch) pita breads

Directions:

In a large bowl, add all ingredients except pita breads and gently toss to coat well.

Arrange pita breads onto serving plates.

Place veggie mixture in the center of each pita bread evenly. Roll the pita bread and serve.

Nutrition	Calories	120	Fat	2.7g	Carbs	20.7g	Protein	3.3g	Sodium	164mg	Phosphorus	63mg	Potassium	164mg

55. Crunchy Veggie Wraps

Preparation Time: 60 minutes | Cooking Time: 15 minutes | Servings: 6

Ingredients:

- ¾ cup of shredded purple cabbage
- ¾ cup of shredded green cabbage
- ½ cup of peeled and julienned cucumber
- ½ cup of peeled and julienned carrot
- ¼ cup of chopped walnuts

- 2 tbsp. of olive oil
- 1 tbsp. of fresh lemon juice
- Pinch of salt
- Freshly ground black pepper, to taste
- 6 medium butter lettuce leaves

Directions:

In a large bowl, add all ingredients except lettuce and toss to coat well.

Place the lettuce leaves onto serving plates. Divide the veggie mixture over each leaf evenly. Top with tofu sauce and serve.

Nutrition	Calories	42	Fat	3.2g	Carbs	3g	Protein	1.6g	Sodium	10mg	Phosphorus	74mg	Potassium	109mg

56. Surprisingly Tasty Chicken Wraps

Preparation Time: 50 minutes | Cooking Time: 15 minutes | Servings: 4

Ingredients:

- 4-ounce of cut into strips unsalted cooked chicken breast
- ½ cup of hulled and thinly sliced fresh strawberries

- 1 thinly sliced English cucumber
- 1 tbsp. of chopped fresh mint leaves
- 4 large lettuce leaves

Directions:

In a large bowl, add all ingredients except lettuce leaves and gently toss to coat well.

Place the lettuce leaves onto serving plates.

Divide the chicken mixture over each leaf evenly and serve immediately.

Nutrition	Calories	74	Fat	2.3g	Carbs	4.7g	Protein	8.3g	Sodium	27mg	Phosphorus	59mg	Potassium	239mg

57. Authentic Shrimp Wraps

Preparation Time: 20 minutes | Cooking Time: 15 minutes | Servings: 4

Ingredients:

- For Filling:
- 1 tbsp. of olive oil
- 1 minced garlic clove
- 1 seeded and chopped medium red bell pepper
- ½ pound of peeled, deveined and chopped medium shrimp
- Pinch of salt
- Freshly ground black pepper, to taste
- For Wraps:
- 4 large lettuce leaves

Directions:

In a large skillet, heat oil on medium heat.

Add garlic and sauté for about 30 seconds.

Add bell pepper and cook for about 2-3 minutes.

Add shrimp and seasoning and cook for about 2-3 minutes.

Remove from heat and cool slightly.

Divide shrimp mixture over lettuce leaves evenly.

Serve immediately.

Nutrition	Calories	97	Fat	4.3g	Carbs	2g	Protein	12.3g	Sodium	169mg	Phosphorus	59mg	Potassium	81mg

58. Loveable Tortillas

Preparation Time: 60 minutes | Cooking Time: 15 minutes | Servings: 8

Ingredients:

- ½ cup of low-sodium mayonnaise
- 1 finely minced small garlic clove
- 8-ounce of chopped unsalted cooked chicken
- ½ of seeded and chopped red bell pepper
- ½ of seeded and chopped green bell pepper
- 1 chopped red onion
- 4 (6-ounce) warmed corn tortillas

Directions:

In a bowl, mix together mayonnaise and garlic.

In another bowl, mix together chicken and vegetables.

Arrange the tortillas onto smooth surface.

Spread mayonnaise mixture over each tortilla evenly.

Place chicken mixture over ¼ of each tortilla.

Fold the outside edges inward and roll up like a burrito.

Secure each tortilla with toothpicks to secure the filling.

Cut each tortilla in half and serve.

Nutrition	Calories	296	Fat	8.2g	Carbs	44g	Protein	13.5g	Sodium	171mg	Phosphorus	99mg	Potassium	269mg

59. Elegant Veggie Tortillas

Preparation Time: 30 minutes | *Cooking Time*: 15 minutes | *Servings*: 12

Ingredients:

- 1½ cups of chopped broccoli florets
- 1½ cups of chopped cauliflower florets
- 1 tbsp. of water
- 2 tsp. of canola oil
- 1½ cups of chopped onion
- 1 minced garlic clove
- 2 tbsp. of finely chopped fresh parsley
- 1 cup of low-cholesterol liquid egg substitute
- Freshly ground black pepper, to taste
- 4 (6-ounce) warmed corn tortillas

Directions:

In a microwave bowl, place broccoli, cauliflower and water and microwave, covered for about 3-5 minutes.

Remove from microwave and drain any liquid.

In a skillet, heat oil on medium heat. Add onion and sauté for about 4-5 minutes.

Add garlic and sauté for about 1 minute. Stir in broccoli, cauliflower, parsley, egg substitute and black pepper.

Reduce the heat to medium-low and simmer for about 10 minutes.

Remove from heat and keep aside to cool slightly. Place broccoli mixture over ¼ of each tortilla.

Fold the outside edges inward and roll up like a burrito. Secure each tortilla with toothpicks to secure the filling. Cut each tortilla in half and serve.

Nutrition	Calories	217	Fat	32g	Carbs	21g	Protein	8.3g	Sodium	87mg	Phosphorus	59mg	Potassium	289mg

60. Delightful Pizza

Preparation Time: 40 minutes | *Cooking Time*: 15 minutes | *Servings*: 4

Ingredients:

- 2 (6½-inch) pita breads
- 3 tbsp. of low-sodium tomato sauce
- 3-ounce of cubed unsalted cooked chicken
- ¼ cup of chopped onion
- 2 tbsp. of crumbled feta cheese

Directions:

Preheat the oven to 350°F. Grease a baking sheet.

Arrange the pita breads onto prepared baking sheet. Spread the barbecue sauce over each pita bread evenly.

Top with chicken and onion evenly and sprinkle with cheese. Bake for about 11-13 minutes. Cut each pizza in half and serve.

Nutrition	Calories	133	Fat	2.2g	Carbs	18g	Protein	9.3g	Sodium	271mg	Phosphorus	59mg	Potassium	3mg

61. Winner Kabobs

Preparation Time: 50 minutes | *Cooking Time*: 15 minutes | *Servings*: 6

Ingredients:

- 1 pound of cubed skinless, boneless chicken breast
- 1 seeded and cut into 1-inch pieces medium red bell pepper
- 1 seeded and cut into 1-inch pieces medium green bell pepper
- 20-ounce of cut into 1-inch pieces pineapple
- 1 cut into 1-inch pieces red onion
- 1/3 cup of low-sodium barbecue sauce
- Freshly ground black pepper, to taste

Directions:

Preheat the outdoor grill to medium-high heat. Lightly, grease the grill grate.

Thread chicken, bell peppers, pineapple and onion onto pre-soaked 6 wooden skewers.

Coat all the ingredients with ½ of barbecue sauce and sprinkle with black pepper.

Place the skewers in prepared baking sheet in a single layer. Grill the skewers for about 9-10 minutes, flipping occasionally.

Remove from grill and immediately, coat with remaining barbecue sauce. Serve immediately.

Nutrition	Calories	182	Fat	3g	Carbs	21g	Protein	18.3g	Sodium	185mg	Phosphorus	21mg	Potassium	234mg

62. Tempting Burgers

Preparation Time: 20 minutes | Cooking Time: 15 minutes | Servings: 6

Ingredients:

- 12-ounce of finely chopped unsalted cooked salmon
- ½ cup of minced onion
- 1 minced garlic clove
- 2 tbsp. of chopped fresh parsley
- 1 large egg
- ½ tsp. of paprika
- Freshly ground black pepper, to taste
- 2 tbsp. of olive oil
- 3 cups torn lettuce

Directions:

Preheat the oven to 350°F. Line a baking sheet with parchment paper.

In a large bowl, add all ingredients except oil and mix until well combined.

Make equal sized 12 patties from mixture. Place patties onto prepared baking dish in a single layer.

Bake for about 12-15 minutes. Now, in a large skillet, heat oil on high heat.

Remove salmon burgers from oven and transfer into skillet. Cook for about 1 minute per side.

Divide lettuce in serving plates evenly. Place 2 patties in each plate and serve.

Nutrition	Calories	136	Fat	0.9g	Carbs	2.1g	Protein	12.4g	Sodium	31mg	Phosphorus	59mg	Potassium	295mg

63. Caraway Cabbage And Rice

Preparation Time: 5 minutes | Cooking Time: 10 minutes | Servings: 2

Ingredients:

- 1 cup of rice, cooked
- ¼ cup mandarin oranges
- 1 tablespoon white onion, chopped
- 1 cup cabbage, shredded
- ½ teaspoon caraway seed
- 1 tablespoon Worcestershire sauce
- ¼ cup water

Directions:

Take a frying pan, grease it with oil, place it over medium heat, add onion and cabbage and cook for 5 minutes until cabbage leaves wilted.

Stir in caraway seeds,

Worcestershire sauce, and water, continue cooking for 3 minutes, add oranges and stir until rice until well combined.

Serve straight away.

Nutrition	Calories	142	Fat	0g	Carbs	31g	Protein	3g	Sodium	71mg	Phosphorus	59mg	Potassium	209mg

64. Gratin Pasta With Watercress And Chicken

Preparation Time: 10 minutes | *Cooking Time: 50 minutes* | *Servings: 4*

Ingredients:

- 2 cups pasta shells, cooked
- 1 cup chicken, shredded and cooked
- 1 small white onion, peeled and chopped
- 1 cup fresh watercress
- 1 teaspoon minced garlic
- ¼ teaspoon ground black pepper
- 1 tablespoon olive oil
- ½ cup Parmesan cheese, grated
- 1 2/3 cup béchamel sauce

Directions:

Take a medium-sized skillet pan, place it over medium heat, add oil and when hot, add onion and garlic, and cook for 4 minutes until saluted.

Then stir in chicken and watercress until mixed and continue cooking for 3 minutes until leaves of watercress have wilted.

Add pasta, pour in half of the béchamel sauce, mix until coated, and spoon the mixture into a greased baking dish.

Cover pasta with remaining béchamel sauce, sprinkle cheese on top and bake for 40 minutes until cheese has melts and pasta is bubbling.

Serve straight away.

Nutrition	Calories	345	Fat	13g	Carbs	38g	Protein	19g	Sodium	101mg	Phosphorus	39mg	Potassium	209mg

65. Orzo And Vegetables

Preparation Time: 5 minutes | *Cooking Time: 10 minutes* | *Servings: 6*

Ingredients:

- 1 medium carrot, peeled and shredded
- 1 small white onion, peeled and chopped
- 1 small zucchini, chopped
- ½ cup frozen green peas
- ½ teaspoon minced garlic
- ¼ teaspoon salt
- ¼ teaspoon ground black pepper
- 1 teaspoon curry powder
- 2 tablespoons olive oil
- ¼ cup Parmesan cheese, grated
- 3 cups chicken broth, low sodium
- 2 tablespoons parsley, chopped
- 1 cup orzo pasta, uncooked

Directions:

Take a large skillet pan, place it over medium heat, add oil and when hot, add onion, garlic, carrot, and zucchini and cook for 5 minutes until sautéed.

Stir in salt and curry powder, pour in the broth, stir until mixed and bring the mixture to a bowl.

Then stir in pasta, bring it to a boil, switch heat to medium-low level, and simmer for 10 minutes all the liquid has absorbed by the pasta.

Stir in remaining ingredients until mixed and cook for 3 minutes, or until hot. Serve straight away.

Nutrition	Calories	176	Fat	4g	Carbs	25g	Protein	10g	Sodium	142mg	Phosphorus	17mg	Potassium	1979mg

66. Lemon Rice With Vegetables

Preparation Time: 5 minutes | *Cooking Time: 35 minutes* | *Servings: 5*

Ingredients:

- 10 tablespoons white rice, uncooked
- 1 ½ cups mushrooms, sliced
- ½ cup celery, sliced
- ¼ cup white onion, chopped

- 1/8 teaspoon ground black pepper
- 1/8 teaspoon dried thyme
- 1/8 teaspoon herb seasoning
- 1 teaspoon grated lemon zest
- 3 tablespoons unsalted margarine
- 2 tablespoons lemon juice
- 1 ¼ cups water

Directions:

Take a large skillet pan, place it over medium heat, add 1 ½ tablespoons margarine and when it melts, add onion and celery and cook for 5 minutes.

Season vegetables with lemon zest, black pepper, thyme, and herb seasoning, stir in water and lemon juice, bring to a boil, stir in rice, bring the mixture, then switch heat to medium-low level and simmer for 20 minutes until rice is tender.

Meanwhile, take a small-sized skillet pan, place it over medium heat, add remaining margarine and when it melts, add mushrooms and cook for 5 minutes until tender.

When the rice has cooked, stir cooked mushrooms in it and serve immediately.

Nutrition	Calories	183	Fat	7g	Carbs	27g	Protein	3g	Sodium	11mg	Phosphorus	102mg	Potassium	309mg

67. Chicken And Asparagus Pasta

Preparation Time: 5 minutes | Cooking Time: 20 minutes | Servings: 8

Ingredients:

- 8 ounces skinless chicken breasts, cubed
- 16 ounces penne pasta, cooked
- 1-pound asparagus spears, trimmed
- ½ teaspoon minced garlic
- ¼ teaspoon garlic powder
- ½ teaspoon ground black pepper
- 1 ½ teaspoons dried oregano
- 5 tablespoons olive oil
- ¼ cup feta cheese, crumbled
- ½ cup chicken broth, low sodium

Directions:

Take a large skillet pan, place it over medium-high heat, add 3 tablespoons oil and when hot, add chicken cubes, stir in garlic powder and ¼ teaspoon black pepper and continue cooking for 5 minutes until cooked and browned.

When done, transfer chicken cubes to a plate lined with paper towels, then pour in chicken broth, add asparagus, season with oregano and remaining black pepper, and cook for 5 minutes until asparagus has steamed, covering the pan.

Then stir in chicken, cook for 3 minutes until warmed, stir in pasta, stir until mixed and cook for 5 minutes until hot.

Set aside until needed.

Drizzle with remaining oil, top with cheese, and serve.

Nutrition	Calories	376	Fat	12g	Carbs	49g	Protein	18g	Sodium	71mg	Phosphorus	59mg	Potassium	209mg

68. Hawaiian Rice

Preparation Time: 5 minutes | Cooking Time: 13 minutes | Servings: 6

Ingredients:

- ½ cup pineapple tidbits, unsweetened
- ½ cup red bell pepper, chopped
- ½ cup mushrooms, chopped
- 1 teaspoon ginger root, minced
- ½ cup bean sprouts
- ½ tablespoon soy sauce, reduced sodium
- ¼ teaspoon salt
- 2 cups brown rice, cooked

Directions:

Take a frying pan, spray it with oil, place it over medium heat and when hot, add all the vegetables and cook for 5 minutes until sautéed.

Then stir in ginger and pineapple, drizzle with soy sauce, season with salt and cook for 3 minutes, or until hot.

Stir in rice until well mixed, cook for 3 minutes until hot, and then serve.

Nutrition	Calories	97	Fat	1g	Carbs	21g	Protein	2g	Sodium	31mg	Phosphorus	79mg	Potassium	29mg

69. Mexican Rice

Preparation Time: 10 minutes | Cooking Time: 30 minutes | Servings: 6

Ingredients:

- ¼ cup white onion, chopped
- ½ teaspoon minced garlic
- ¼ teaspoon salt
- ¼ cup canola oil
- ¼ cup tomato sauce, low sodium
- 3 cups of water
- 1 cup white rice, uncooked

Directions:

Take a medium-sized skillet pan, place it over medium-high heat, add oil and when hot, add rice and cook for 5 minutes until browned.

Then add onion and garlic, stir until mixed, and cook for 3 minutes, or until tender.

Season with salt, pour in tomato sauce and water, stir until mixed, simmer for 20 minutes until rice has cooked, covering the pan. Serve straight away.

Nutrition	Calories	194	Fat	12g	Carbs	24g	Protein	2g	Sodium	41mg	Phosphorus	89mg	Potassium	209mg

70. Shrimp Fried Rice

Preparation Time: 5 minutes | Cooking Time: 20 minutes | Servings: 4

Ingredients:

- 4 cups white rice, cooked
- ½ cup small frozen shrimp, cooked
- ¾ cup white onion, chopped
- 1 cup frozen peas and carrots
- 3 tablespoons scallions, chopped
- ½ teaspoon minced garlic
- 1 tablespoon ginger root, grated
- ¼ teaspoon salt
- ¾ teaspoon ground black pepper
- 5 tablespoons peanut oil
- 4 eggs

Directions:

Take a large skillet pan, place it over medium-high heat, add 1 tablespoon peanut oil and when hot, add onion, season with ½ teaspoon black pepper, and cook for 2 minutes, or until onions are tender.

Stir in scallions, ginger, and garlic, cook for 1 minute, add shrimps, stir until mixed, cook for 2 minutes until hot, then stir in carrots and peas and cook for 2 minutes until hot.

When done, transfer shrimps and vegetable mixture to a bowl, cover with a lid and set aside until required.

Return the skillet pan over medium heat, add 2 tablespoons oil, beat the eggs, pour it into the pan, cook for 3 minutes until eggs are scrambled to desired level and then transfer eggs to the bowl containing shrimps and vegetables.

Add remaining 1 tablespoon oil and when hot, add rice, stir until well coated, and cook for 2 minutes until hot.

Then season rice with salt and remaining black pepper, cook for 2 minutes, don't stir, then add eggs, shrimps, and vegetables, stir until mixed and cook for 3 minutes until hot. Serve straight away.

Nutrition	Calories	421	Fat	16g	Carbs	53g	Protein	16.3g	Sodium	109mg	Phosphorus	179mg	Potassium	319mg

71. Vegetarian Egg Fried Rice

Preparation Time: 5 minutes | *Cooking Time: 18 minutes* | *Servings: 6*

Ingredients:

- 4 cups white rice, cooked
- 1 cup diced tofu, extra-firm, drained
- ½ cup green onion, chopped
- 1 cup white onion, diced
- 1 cup fresh carrots, sliced
- ½ cup green peas
- 1 tablespoon ginger root, grated
- 1 teaspoon minced garlic
- ¼ teaspoon mustard powder
- ½ cup cilantro, chopped
- 3 tablespoons canola oil
- 1 tablespoon soy sauce, reduced sodium
- 6 eggs, beaten

Directions:

Take a large skillet pan, place it over medium heat, add oil and when hot, add beaten eggs and cook the omelet for 3 minutes until eggs are cooked to the desired level.

Transfer omelet to a cutting board, let it cool for 5 minutes, and chop it, set aside until needed.

Add oil in the pan and when hot, add all the vegetables, stir in tofu, garlic, and ginger, season with mustard, cook for 5 minutes until carrots have softened.

Stir in rice and chopped eggs, drizzle with soy sauce, stir until well mixed and remove the pan from heat.

Garnish rice with green onion and cilantro and then serve.

Nutrition	Calories	334	Fat	15g	Carbs	37g	Protein	17.3g	Sodium	171mg	Phosphorus	101mg	Potassium	109mg

72 Autumn Orzo Salad

Preparation Time: 35 minutes | *Cooking Time: 0 minutes* | *Servings: 4*

Ingredients:

- 1 medium apple, cored and diced
- ¾ cups orzo, cooked
- ¼ teaspoon ground black pepper
- 1 tablespoon fresh basil, chopped
- 2 tablespoons lemon juice
- 2 tablespoons olive oil
- 2 tablespoons almonds, sliced and blanched

Directions:

Take a medium-sized bowl, add all the ingredients in it (except for almonds), and stir until incorporated.

Take a baking dish, place prepared mixture in it, and place in the refrigerator for 30 minutes until chilled.

When ready to eat, garnish with almonds and serve.

Nutrition	Calories	227	Fat	9g	Carbs	29g	Protein	5g	Sodium	12mg	Phosphorus	159mg	Potassium	27mg

73 Green Pepper Slaw

Preparation Time: 5 minutes | *Cooking Time: 0 minutes* | *Servings: 12*

Ingredients:

- 2 medium carrots, peeled and chopped
- 1 small head of cabbage, chopped
- 1 medium green bell pepper, cored and chopped
- 2 teaspoons celery seed
- ½ cup Splenda granulated sugar
- ½ cup apple cider vinegar
- ½ cup water

Directions:

Take a salad bowl, place carrot, cabbage, and bell pepper in it and mix well until combined.

Whisk together celery seeds, sugar, vinegar, and water until blended, drizzle it over the salad and toss until mixed. Serve straight away.

Nutrition	Calories	76	Fat	0g	Carbs	18g	Protein	1g	Sodium	12mg	Phosphorus	59mg	Potassium	109mg

74. Easy Lemon Butter Salmon
Preparation Time: 5 minutes | Cooking Time: 15 minutes | Servings: 5

Ingredients:

- 2 teaspoons minced garlic
- 1/2 cup butter, cubed
- 6 tablespoons lemon juice
- 2 teaspoons salt
- 1/2 teaspoon pepper
- 1/2 teaspoon hot pepper sauce
- 5 salmon fillets or steaks (6 ounces each)

Directions:

In a small skillet, sauté garlic in butter; whisk in lemon juice, salt, pepper and pepper sauce. Transfer 2/3 cup to a serving bowl; set aside. Place salmon in a greased 15x10x1-in. baking pan.

Drizzle with remaining lemon butter. Broil 4-6 in. from heat 10-15 minutes or until fish flakes easily with a fork. Serve with reserved lemon butter.

Nutrition	Calories	479	Fat	37g	Carbs	1g	Protein	34g	Sodium	1177mg	Phosphorus	59mg	Potassium	209mg

75. Perfect Grilled Skirt Steak
Preparation Time: 15 minutes | Cooking Time: 10 minutes | Servings: 4-6

Ingredients:

- 1/4 cup canola oil
- 1/4 cup Meat Seasoning*
- 2 tablespoons garlic, chopped
- 2 tablespoons lemon juice, fresh
- 2 pounds skirt steak, trimmed
- Meat Seasoning
- Makes about 1/4 cup
- 2 tablespoons freshly ground black pepper
- 1 tablespoon salt
- 1 teaspoon ground cinnamon
- 1/2 teaspoon paprika
- 1/2 teaspoon dried thyme
- 1/2 teaspoon granulated onion powder
- 1/2 teaspoon granulated garlic powder
- 1/4 teaspoon ground cumin

Directions:

In a small bowl, stir together the pepper, salt, cinnamon, paprika, thyme, onion powder, garlic powder, and cumin. Store the seasoning in a lidded glass container or zipped plastic bag in a cool, dark place for up to 1 month.

For the Steak: In a small bowl, mix together the oil, seasoning, garlic, and lemon juice. Rub the mixture on both sides of the meat, making sure to work it into the meat.

Let the meat marinate at room temperature for at least 30 minutes but no longer than 45 minutes (if the day is very hot, don't leave the meat out for longer than 30 minutes).

Prepare a hot fire in a charcoal or gas grill and oil the grill grates.

Grill the steak for 3 to 5 minutes on each side, until done to the degree of doneness you prefer.

Let the skirt steaks rest for 5 minutes before slicing to serve.

Nutrition	Calories	200	Fat	12g	Carbs	3g	Protein	20g	Sodium	190mg	Phosphorus	65mg	Potassium	310mg

76. Lamb Curry Stew with Artichoke Hearts

*Preparation Time: 10 minutes | **Cooking Time**: 1 hours and 20 minutes | **Servings**: 4*

Ingredients:

- ½ teaspoon black pepper
- ½ teaspoon curry powder
- ½ teaspoon ground cinnamon
- 1 clove garlic, minced
- 2 cups of beef broth
- 2 cups of water
- 2 tablespoons onion powder
- 1 tablespoon curry powder
- 1 tablespoon fresh lemon juice
- 1 tablespoon olive oil
- 1 teaspoon garam masala
- 1 teaspoon salt
- 1/3 cup manzanilla olives
- 14 ½ ounce fire roasted diced tomatoes
- 14-ounces artichoke hearts, quartered
- 2 teaspoon ginger root, grated
- 2-pounds lamb leg, trimmed from fat and cut into chunks

Directions:

In a bowl, combine the lamb meat with salt, pepper and ½ tablespoon of curry.

Place a heavy bottomed pot on medium high fire and heat for 2 minutes.

Add oil and heat for 2 minutes. Add lamb meat and sauté until all sides are brown. Remove from the pot and set aside.

Sauté garlic and ginger for a minute or two.

Pour the broth and scrape the sides or bottoms from the browning. Add the lamb back and place the rest of the ingredients except for the lemon juice.

Cover and bring to a boil. Boil for 10 minutes. Lower fire to a simmer and simmer until fork tender, around 60 minutes.

Add the lemon juice and let it rest for 5 minutes before serving.

Nutrition	Calories	436	Fat	18g	Carbs	19g	Protein	7.3g	Sodium	1471mg	Phosphorus	259mg	Potassium	1417mg

77. Beef Chow Mein in Zucchini Noodles

*Preparation Time: 10 minutes | **Cooking Time**: 1 hours and 20 minutes | **Servings**: 4*

Ingredients:

- 2 zucchinis, processed into spaghetti-like noodles
- 1 egg omelet, julienned
- ¼ cup cilantro, minced
- For the Beef
- 2 teaspoons sugar
- 1 teaspoon sea salt
- 1 tablespoon dark soy sauce
- 1 pound round steak, julienned
- For the Stir Fry
- 4 fresh shiitake mushrooms, caps julienned
- 4 leeks, sliced into inch-long slivers
- 2 tablespoons cornstarch, dissolved in 2 tablespoons water
- 1½ tablespoons peanut or coconut oil
- 2 cups low-sodium vegetable stock
- 1-pound fresh bean sprouts
- 1 can bamboo shoot strip

Directions:

Place beef and marinade ingredients into a large food-safe bag; seal. Massage contents of bag to combine.

Marinate in fridge for at least 30 minutes prior to use (or up to 42 hours before hand.) Drain well; reserve marinade for later.

Pour ½ tablespoon of oil into large nonstick wok set over medium heat; stir-fry zoodles until lightly seared.

Transfer to plate lined with paper towels to remove excess moisture. Set aside.

Pour ½ tablespoon of oil into same wok.

Cooking in batches, stir-fry half of marinated beef until brown on all sides; transfer to a plate.

Repeat step for remaining beef.

Return beef to wok, along with beef stock, cornstarch slurry, reserved marinade, and mushrooms.

Boil; continue cooking until mushrooms are fork-tender.

Except for garnishes, add remaining ingredients into wok, including zoodles.

Stir-fry until bean sprouts wilt, about 20 seconds.

Turn off heat.

Spoon equal portions of chow mein on a plate; garnish with cilantro and sliced egg. Serve.

Nutrition	Calories	376	Fat	1.8g	Carbs	2.1g	Protein	47.3g	Sodium	543mg	Phosphorus	59mg	Potassium	209mg

78. Mint Pesto Zucchini Noodles

Preparation Time: 10 minutes | Cooking Time: 15 minutes | Servings: 4

Ingredients:

- 1/4 cup sliced almonds, toasted
- 1 cup mint leaves
- 1/4 cup fresh dill
- 1 clove of garlic, chopped
- 1/4 cup extra-virgin olive oil
- 1/4 cup grated Parmesan cheese
- 2 tbsp lemon juice
- Salt and pepper to taste
- 3 medium zucchini

Directions:

For the almonds:

Heat oven to 350°F. Place slivered almonds in a single layer on a baking sheet, and toast for 8 minutes, or until they have browned slightly and just become fragrant.

Remove the sheet from the oven and immediately place almonds on a plate or in a bowl.

For the mint pesto:

Add mint leaves, dill, and garlic to the bowl of a food processor and process until the herbs are finely broken up.

Add olive oil, Parmesan, lemon juice, and salt and pepper and process until creamy.

For the zucchini noodles:

Slice the very ends off of three zucchini and spiralize using the fine spiralizer blade (or your blade of choice).

Add the zucchini noodles to a large mixing bowl and pour in the pesto sauce. Toss to combine.

Top with additional Parmesan, dill, mint, and/or toasted almonds for serving.

Nutrition	Calories	169	Fat	15g	Carbs	6.5g	Protein	4.3g	Sodium	150mg	Phosphorus	129mg	Potassium	319mg

79. Beef Shanghai Rolls

Preparation Time: 10 minutes | Cooking Time: 1 hours and 20 minutes | Servings: 4

Ingredients:

- 4 tablespoons hot or sweet chili sauce, as dipping sauce
- 1 package rice paper wrapper, large
- Water for sealing
- Oil for deep frying
- For the Filling
- 1 pound lean ground beef
- 1 shallot, minced
- 1 carrot, minced

- 1 garlic clove, grated
- 1 tablespoon low-sodium soy sauce
- 1 tablespoon fresh parsley, minced
- ½ cup butternut squash, minced
- ¼ cup fresh chives, minced
- ¼ cup sweet potato, minced
- Pinch of black pepper

Directions:

Mix filling ingredients in a bowl.

Spoon 1 heaped tablespoon of filling in middle of spring roll wrapper; pinch and pull filling until you have a relatively straight but thin line that runs from one corner of wrapper to the other, leaving only an inch of space at the ends.

Dampen remaining edges with water. Fold wrapper over; start rolling tightly, leaving side edges open.

Pinch edges; slice off parts that don't contain any filling.

Divide each spring roll in half. Repeat step for remaining fillings/wrappers.

Half fill deep fryer with oil; set at medium heat.

When oil becomes slightly smoky, reduce heat to lowest setting; gently slide in spring rolls a few pieces at a time.

Cook for 15 minutes; wrapper should be light brown. (If it becomes too dark, your heat setting is too high.

Turn down heat immediately.) Transfer cooked pieces to a plate lined with paper towels.

Place recommended number of pieces onto plates. Serve with hot or sweet chili sauce on the side.

Nutrition	Calories	145	Fat	4.2g	Carbs	2.1g	Protein	37.3g	Sodium	285mg	Phosphorus	59mg	Potassium	605mg

80. Roasted Wedges of Cabbage

Preparation Time: 12 minutes | Cooking Time: 35 minutes | Servings: 16

Ingredients:

- 2 tsp sugar
- 1 green cabbage, cut into 1-in wedges
- 1 tbsp balsamic vinegar

- ¼ tsp freshly ground pepper
- 2 tbsp olive oil

Directions:

Preheat oven to 450°F, with baking pan heating inside.

Combine sugar and pepper in a small bowl.

Brush cabbage wedges with oil. Sprinkle with pepper and sugar.

Put the seasoned wedges on the hot baking sheet. Roast until cabbage is browned and tender for 25 minutes.

Drizzle with balsamic vinegar.

Nutrition	Calories	32	Fat	1.8g	Carbs	4g	Protein	0.3g	Sodium	41mg	Phosphorus	29mg	Potassium	109mg

81. Green Bean Garlic Salad

Preparation Time: 5 minutes | Cooking Time: 20 minutes | Servings: 4

Ingredients:

- 2 cloves garlic, chopped
- 2 cups green beans
- 1 tbsp sesame oil
- 1 tbsp balsamic or red wine vinegar

Directions:

Clean the beans. Cook them in boiling water until tender.

Drain and cool them under cold water.

Toss the beans with the oil, vinegar, and garlic.

Nutrition	Calories	59	Fat	6g	Carbs	6g	Protein	1.3g	Sodium	12mg	Phosphorus	159mg	Potassium	29mg

82. Classic Chicken Soup

Preparation Time: 5-10 minutes | Cooking Time: 35 minutes | Servings: 6

Ingredients:

- 2 teaspoons minced garlic
- 2 celery stalks, chopped
- 1 tablespoon unsalted butter
- ½ sweet onion, diced
- 1 carrot, diced
- 4 cups of water
- 1 teaspoon chopped fresh thyme
- 2 cups chopped cooked chicken breast
- 1 cup chicken stock
- Black pepper (ground), to taste
- 2 tablespoons chopped fresh parsley

Directions:

Take a medium-large cooking pot, heat oil over medium heat.

Add onion and stir-cook until become translucent and softened.

Add garlic and stir-cook until you become fragrant.

Add celery, carrot, chicken, chicken stock, and water. Boil the mixture.

Over low heat, simmer the mixture for about 25-30 minutes until veggies are tender.

Mix in thyme and cook for 2 minutes.

Season to taste with black pepper. Serve warm with parsley on top.

Nutrition	Calories	436	Fat	8g	Carbs	2g	Protein	15.3g	Sodium	74mg	Phosphorus	129mg	Potassium	209mg

83. Creamy Penne

Preparation Time: 10 minutes | Cooking Time: 25 minutes | Servings: 4

Ingredients:

- ½ cup penne, dried
- 9 oz chicken fillet
- 1 teaspoon Italian seasoning
- 1 tablespoon olive oil
- 1 tomato, chopped
- 1 cup heavy cream
- 1 tablespoon fresh basil, chopped
- ½ teaspoon salt
- 2 oz Parmesan, grated
- 1 cup water, for cooking

63

Directions:

Pour water in the pan, add penne, and boil it for 15 minutes. Then drain water.

Pour olive oil in the skillet and heat it up.

Slice the chicken fillet and put it in the hot oil.

Sprinkle chicken with Italian seasoning and roast for 2 minutes from each side.

Then add fresh basil, salt, tomato, and grated cheese.

Stir well. Add heavy cream and cooked penne.

Cook the meal for 5 minutes more over the medium heat. Stir it from time to time.

Nutrition	Calories	388	Fat	23.4g	Carbs	17.6g	Protein	17.3g	Sodium	71mg	Phosphorus	59mg	Potassium	209mg

84. Light Paprika Moussaka

Preparation Time: 15 minutes Cooking Time: 45 minutes Servings: 3

Ingredients:

- 1 eggplant, trimmed
- 1 cup ground chicken
- 1/3 cup white onion, diced
- 3 oz Cheddar cheese, shredded
- 1 potato, sliced
- 1 teaspoon olive oil
- 1 teaspoon salt
- ½ cup milk
- 1 tablespoon butter
- 1 tablespoon ground paprika
- 1 tablespoon Italian seasoning
- 1 teaspoon tomato paste

Directions:

Slice the eggplant lengthwise and sprinkle with salt. Pour olive oil in the skillet and add sliced potato.

Roast potato for 2 minutes from each side. Then transfer it in the plate.

Put eggplant in the skillet and roast it for 2 minutes from each side too.

Pour milk in the pan and bring it to boil. Add tomato paste, Italian seasoning, paprika, butter, and Cheddar cheese.

Then mix up together onion with ground chicken. Arrange the sliced potato in the casserole in one layer.

Then add ½ part of all sliced eggplants. Spread the eggplants with ½ part of chicken mixture.

Then add remaining eggplants. Pour the milk mixture over the eggplants. Bake moussaka for 30 minutes at 355°F.

Nutrition	Calories	378	Fat	21g	Carbs	12g	Protein	25.7g	Sodium	171mg	Phosphorus	259mg	Potassium	359mg

85. Cucumber Bowl with Spices and Greek Yogurt

Preparation Time: 10 minutes | Cooking Time: 20 minutes | Servings: 3

Ingredients:

- 4 cucumbers
- ½ teaspoon chili pepper
- ¼ cup fresh parsley, chopped
- ¾ cup fresh dill, chopped
- 2 tablespoons lemon juice
- ½ teaspoon salt
- ½ teaspoon ground black pepper
- ¼ teaspoon sage
- ½ teaspoon dried oregano
- 1/3 cup Greek yogurt

Directions:

Make the cucumber dressing: blend the dill and parsley until you get green mash.

Then combine together green mash with lemon juice, salt, ground black pepper, sage, dried oregano, Greek yogurt, and chili pepper.

Churn the mixture well. Chop the cucumbers roughly and combine them with cucumber dressing. Mix up well. Refrigerate the cucumber for 20 minutes.

Nutrition	Calories	114	Fat	1.6g	Carbs	12g	Protein	7.7g	Sodium	71mg	Phosphorus	159mg	Potassium	147mg

86. Stuffed Bell Peppers with Quinoa
Preparation Time: 10 minutes | Cooking Time: 35 minutes | Servings: 2

Ingredients:

- 2 bell peppers
- 1/3 cup quinoa
- 3 oz chicken stock
- ¼ cup onion, diced
- ½ teaspoon salt
- ¼ teaspoon tomato paste
- ½ teaspoon dried oregano
- 1/3 cup sour cream
- 1 teaspoon paprika

Directions:

Trim the bell peppers and remove the seeds. Then combine together chicken stock and quinoa in the pan.

Add salt and boil the ingredients for 10 minutes or until quinoa will soak all liquid.

Then combine together cooked quinoa with dried oregano, tomato paste, and onion.

Fill the bell peppers with the quinoa mixture and arrange in the casserole mold.

Add sour cream and bake the peppers for 25 minutes at 365°F.

Serve the cooked peppers with sour cream sauce from the casserole mold.

Nutrition	Calories	237	Fat	10g	Carbs	31g	Protein	5.7g	Sodium	51mg	Phosphorus	59mg	Potassium	219mg

87. Mediterranean Burrito
Preparation Time: 10 minutes | Cooking Time: 30 minutes | Servings: 2

Ingredients:

- 2 wheat tortillas
- 2 oz red kidney beans, canned, drained
- 2 tablespoons hummus
- 2 teaspoons tahini sauce
- 1 cucumber
- 2 lettuce leaves
- 1 tablespoon lime juice
- 1 teaspoon olive oil
- ½ teaspoon dried oregano

Directions:

Mash the red kidney beans until you get a puree.

Then spread the wheat tortillas with beans mash from one side. Add hummus and tahini sauce.

Cut the cucumber into the wedges and place them over tahini sauce. Then add lettuce leaves.

Make the dressing: mix up together olive oil, dried oregano, and lime juice.

Drizzle the lettuce leaves with the dressing and wrap the wheat tortillas in the shape of burritos.

Nutrition	Calories	288	Fat	14g	Carbs	38g	Protein	12.3g	Sodium	132mg	Phosphorus	170mg	Potassium	199mg

88. Sweet Potato Bacon Mash

Preparation Time: 10 minutes | Cooking Time: 20 minutes | Servings: 4

Ingredients:

- 3 sweet potato, peeled
- 4 oz bacon, chopped
- 1 cup chicken stock
- 1 tablespoon butter
- 1 teaspoon salt
- 2 oz Parmesan, grated

Directions:

Chop sweet potato and put it in the pan.

Add chicken stock and close the lid.

Boil the vegetables for 15 minutes or until they are soft. After this, drain the chicken stock.

Mash the sweet potato with the help of the potato masher. Add grated cheese and butter.

Mix up together salt and chopped bacon. Fry the mixture until it is crunchy (10-15 minutes).

Add cooked bacon in the mashed sweet potato and mix up with the help of the spoon.

It is recommended to serve the meal warm or hot.

Nutrition	Calories	340	Fat	18.1g	Carbs	18g	Protein	17g	Sodium	210mg	Phosphorus	39mg	Potassium	103mg

89. Prosciutto Wrapped Mozzarella Balls

Preparation Time: 10 minutes | Cooking Time: 10 minutes | Servings: 4

Ingredients:

- 8 Mozzarella balls, cherry size
- 4 oz bacon, sliced
- ¼ teaspoon ground black pepper
- ¾ teaspoon dried rosemary
- 1 teaspoon butter

Directions:

Sprinkle the sliced bacon with ground black pepper and dried rosemary.

Wrap every Mozzarella ball in the sliced bacon and secure them with toothpicks. Melt butter.

Brush wrapped Mozzarella balls with butter.

Line the tray with the baking paper and arrange Mozzarella balls in it.

Bake the meal for 10 minutes at 365°F.

Nutrition	Calories	323	Fat	26g	Carbs	0.6g	Protein	20.7g	Sodium	98mg	Phosphorus	171mg	Potassium	374mg

90. Garlic Chicken Balls

Preparation Time: 15 minutes | Cooking Time: 10 minutes | Servings: 4

Ingredients:

- 2 cups ground chicken
- 1 teaspoon minced garlic
- 1 teaspoon dried dill
- 1/3 carrot, grated
- 1 egg, beaten
- 1 tablespoon olive oil
- ¼ cup coconut flakes
- ½ teaspoon salt

Directions:

In the mixing bowl mix up together ground chicken, minced garlic, dried dill, carrot, egg, and salt.

Stir the chicken mixture with the help of the fingertips until homogenous. Then make medium balls from the mixture.

Coat every chicken ball in coconut flakes.

Heat up olive oil in the skillet.

Add chicken balls and cook them for 3 minutes from each side. The cooked chicken balls will have a golden-brown color.

Nutrition	Calories	200	Fat	11.6g	Carbs	1.2g	Protein	21.7g	Sodium	132mg	Phosphorus	49.3mg	Potassium	198mg

91. Stuffed Tomatoes with Cheese and Meat
Preparation Time: 15 minutes | Cooking Time: 45 minutes | Servings: 4

Ingredients:

- ½ cup ground beef
- ¼ onion, diced
- 1 teaspoon olive oil
- ½ teaspoon salt
- 3 oz Cheddar cheese
- 4 large tomatoes
- 1/3 cup water

Directions:

Pour olive oil in the skillet. Heat it up and add the onion. Cook it for 3 minutes.

Then add ground beef and salt. Stir well.

Cook the meat mixture for 15 minutes over the medium-high heat. Then scoop the meat from the tomatoes.

Fill the tomatoes with ground beef mixture and top with shredded cheese.

Arrange the stuffed tomatoes in the baking tray and add water. Bake the tomatoes for 20 minutes at 350°F.

Nutrition	Calories	164	Fat	10.6g	Carbs	8g	Protein	10.2g	Sodium	191mg	Phosphorus	123mg	Potassium	39mg

92. Stuffed Meatballs with Eggs
Preparation Time: 15 minutes | Cooking Time: 35 minutes | Servings: 4

Ingredients:

- 1 cup ground beef
- ½ cup ground pork
- 4 eggs, boiled, peeled
- 1 tablespoon semolina
- ½ teaspoon salt
- 1 teaspoon chili flakes
- 1 teaspoon turmeric
- ½ teaspoon white pepper
- ½ teaspoon garlic powder
- 1 tablespoon tomato paste
- 1/3 cup water
- 1 teaspoon butter

Directions:

In the mixing bowl, mix up together ground beef and ground pork. Add semolina, salt, chili flakes, salt, chili flakes, turmeric, white pepper, and garlic powder.

Stir the mass until smooth. Then make 4 balls from the meat mixture.

Fill every meatball with a boiled egg. Mix up together water and tomato paste.

Place the meatballs in the casserole mold, add butter and tomato paste mixture. Bake the meatballs for 35 minutes.

Nutrition	Calories	269	Fat	17.6g	Carbs	3.8g	Protein	22.8g	Sodium	320mg	Phosphorus	73mg	Potassium	302mg

93. Beef Okra Soup

Preparation Time: *10 minutes* | ***Cooking Time:*** *45-55 minutes* | ***Servings:*** *6-8*

Ingredients:

- ½ cup okra
- ½ teaspoon basil
- ½ cup carrots, diced
- 3 ½ cups water
- 1 pound beef stew meat
- 1 cup raw sliced onions
- ½ cup green peas
- 1 teaspoon black pepper
- ½ teaspoon thyme
- ½ cup corn kernels

Directions:

Take a medium-large cooking pot, heat oil over medium heat.

Add water, beef stew meat, black pepper, onions, basil, thyme, and stir-cook for 40-45 minutes until meat is tender.

Add all veggies.

Over low heat, simmer the mixture for about 20-25 minutes. Add more water if needed.

Serve soup warm.

Nutrition	Calories	187	Fat	12g	Carbs	7g	Protein	11g	Sodium	59mg	Phosphorus	119mg	Potassium	288mg

94. Green Bean Veggie Stew

Preparation Time: *30 minutes* | ***Cooking Time:*** *35 minutes* | ***Servings:*** *6*

Ingredients:

- 6 cups shredded green cabbage
- 3 celery stalks, chopped
- 1 teaspoon unsalted butter
- ½ large sweet onion, chopped
- 1 teaspoon minced garlic
- 1 scallion, chopped
- 2 tablespoons chopped fresh parsley
- 2 tablespoons lemon juice
- 1 teaspoon chopped fresh oregano
- 1 tablespoon chopped fresh thyme
- 1 teaspoon chopped savory
- Water
- 1 cup fresh green beans, cut into 1-inch pieces
- Black pepper (ground), to taste

Directions:

Take a medium-large cooking pot, heat butter over medium heat.

Add onion and stir-cook until become translucent and softened.

Add garlic and stir-cook until you become fragrant.

Add cabbage, celery, scallion, parsley, lemon juice, thyme, savory, and oregano; add water to cover veggies by 3-4 inches.

Stir the mixture and boil it.

Over low heat, cover, and simmer the mixture for about 25 minutes until veggies are tender.

Add green beans and cook for 2-3 more minutes. Season with black pepper to taste.

Serve warm.

Nutrition	Calories	56	Fat	1g	Carbs	7g	Protein	1g	Sodium	31mg	Phosphorus	36mg	Potassium	197mg

Chapter 6: Dinner Recipes

95. Apple Spice Pork Chops

*Preparation Time: 10 minutes | **Cooking Time:** 10 minutes | **Servings:** 4*

Ingredients:

- 2 medium apples: peeled, cored, sliced
- 1-pound pork chops
- ¼ teaspoon salt
- ¼ cup brown sugar

- ¼ teaspoon ground nutmeg
- ¼ teaspoon ground black pepper
- ¼ teaspoon cinnamon
- 2 tablespoons unsalted butter

Directions:

Switch on the broiler, let it preheat, then place pork chops in it and cook for 5 minutes per side until done.

Meanwhile, take a medium-sized skillet pan, place it over medium heat, add butter and when it melts, add apples, sprinkle with black pepper, salt, sugar, cinnamon, and nutmeg, stir well and cook for 8 minutes, or until apples are tender and the sauce has thickened to the desired level.

When done, spoon the applesauce over pork chops and serve.

Nutrition	Calories	306	Fat	1.6g	Carbs	21g	Protein	22g	Sodium	192mg	Phosphorus	174mg	Potassium	117mg

96. Beef Burritos

*Preparation Time: 10 minutes | **Cooking Time:** 20 minutes | **Servings:** 6*

Ingredients:

- ¼ cup white onion, chopped
- ¼ cup green bell pepper, chopped
- 1-pound ground beef
- ¼ cup tomato puree, low sodium

- ¼ teaspoon ground black pepper
- ¼ teaspoon ground cumin
- 6 flour tortillas, burrito size

Directions:

Take a skillet pan, place it over medium heat and when hot, add beef and cook for 5 to 8 minutes until browned.

Drain the excess fat, then transfer beef to a plate lined with paper towels and serve.

Return pan over medium heat, grease it with oil and when hot, add pepper and onion and cook for 5 minutes, or until softened.

Switch to low heat, return beef to the pan, season with black pepper and cumin, pour in tomato puree, stir until mixed and cook for 5 minutes until done.

Distribute beef mixture evenly on top of the tortilla, roll them in burrito style by folding both ends and then serve.

Nutrition	Calories	265	Fat	9g	Carbs	31g	Protein	15g	Sodium	341mg	Phosphorus	37mg	Potassium	130mg

97. Broccoli And Beef Stir-Fry

*Preparation Time: 5 minutes | **Cooking Time:** 20 minutes | **Servings:** 4*

Ingredients:

- 12 ounces frozen broccoli, thawed
- 8 ounces sirloin beef, cut into thin strips
- 1 medium Roma tomato, chopped
- 1 teaspoon minced garlic

- 1 tablespoon cornstarch
- 2 tablespoons soy sauce, reduced sodium
- ¼ cup chicken broth, low sodium
- 2 tablespoons peanut oil

- 2 cups cooked brown rice

Directions:

Take a frying pan, place it over medium heat, add oil and when hot, add garlic and cook for 1 minute until fragrant.

Add vegetable blend, cook for 5 minutes, then transfer vegetable blend to a plate and set aside until needed.

Add beef strips into the pan, and then cook for 7 minutes until cooked to the desired level.

Prepare the sauce by putting cornstarch in a bowl, and then whisking in soy sauce and broth until well combined.

Returned vegetables to the pan, add tomatoes, drizzle with sauce, stir well until coated, and cook for 2 minutes until the sauce has thickened.

Serve with brown rice.

Nutrition	Calories	373	Fat	16g	Carbs	37g	Protein	18g	Sodium	351mg	Phosphorus	102mg	Potassium	94mg

98. Slow-Cooked Lemon Chicken

Preparation Time: 20 minutes | Cooking Time: 7 hours | Servings: 4

Ingredients:

- 1 teaspoon dried oregano
- ¼ teaspoon ground black pepper
- 2 tablespoons butter, unsalted
- 1-pound chicken breast, boneless, skinless
- ¼ cup chicken broth, low sodium
- ¼ cup water
- 1 tablespoon lemon juice
- 2 cloves garlic, minced
- 1 teaspoon fresh basil, chopped

Directions:

Combine oregano and ground black pepper in a small bowl. Rub mixture on the chicken.

Melt the butter in a medium-sized skillet over medium heat.

Brown the chicken in the melted butter and then transfer the chicken to the slow cooker.

Place chicken broth, water, lemon juice and garlic in the skillet.

Bring it to a boil so it loosens the browned bits from the skillet. Pour over the chicken.

Cover set slow cooker on high for 2½ hours or low for 5 hours.

Add basil and baste chicken. Cover cook on high for an additional 15–30 minutes or until chicken is tender.

Nutrition	Calories	197	Fat	9g	Carbs	1g	Protein	26g	Sodium	57mg	Phosphorus	67mg	Potassium	137mg

99. Pasta With Cheesy Meat Sauce

Preparation Time: 10 minutes | Cooking Time: 30 minutes | Servings: 6

Ingredients:

- ½ box large-shaped pasta
- 1-pound ground beef*
- ½ cup onions, diced
- 1 tablespoon onion flakes
- 1½ cups beef stock, reduced or no sodium
- 1 tablespoon Better Than Bouillon® beef, no salt added
- 1 tablespoon tomato sauce, no salt added
- ¾ cup Monterey or pepper jack cheese, shredded
- 8 ounces cream cheese, softened
- ½ teaspoon Italian seasoning
- ½ teaspoon ground black pepper
- 2 tablespoons French's® Worcestershire sauce, reduced sodium

Directions:

Cook pasta noodles according to the Directions: on the box.

In a large sauté pan, cook ground beef, onions and onion flakes until the meat is browned.

Drain and add stock, bouillon and tomato sauce.

Bring to a simmer, stirring occasionally.

Stir in cooked pasta, turn off heat, and add softened cream cheese, shredded cheese and seasonings (Italian seasoning, black pepper and Worcestershire sauce). Stir pasta mixture until cheese is melted throughout.

TIP: You can substitute ground turkey for beef.

Nutrition	Calories	502	Fat	30g	Carbs	35g	Protein	23g	Sodium	401mg	Phosphorus	359mg	Potassium	247mg

100. Aromatic Herbed Rice

Preparation Time: 10 minutes | Cooking Time: 15 minutes | Servings: 6

Ingredients:

- 2 tablespoons olive oil
- 3 cups cooked rice (don't overcook)
- 4–5 cloves fresh garlic, sliced thin
- 2 tablespoons fresh cilantro, chopped
- 2 tablespoons fresh oregano, chopped
- 2 tablespoons fresh chives, chopped
- ½ teaspoon red pepper flakes
- 1 teaspoon red wine vinegar

Directions:

In a large sauté pan, heat olive oil on medium-high heat and lightly sauté garlic.

Add rice, herbs and red pepper flakes and continue to cook for 2–4 minutes or until well-mixed.

Turn off heat, add vinegar, mix well and serve.

Nutrition	Calories	134	Fat	5g	Carbs	21g	Protein	2g	Sodium	61mg	Phosphorus	37mg	Potassium	89mg

101. Herb-Crusted Roast Leg Of Lamb

Preparation Time: 10 minutes | Cooking Time: 45 minutes | Servings: 12

Ingredients:

- 1 4-pound leg of lamb
- 3 tablespoons lemon juice
- 1 tablespoon curry powder
- 2 cloves garlic, minced
- ½ teaspoon ground black pepper
- 1 cup onions, sliced
- ½ cup dry vermouth

Directions:

Preheat oven to 400° F.

Place leg of lamb on a roasting pan. Sprinkle with 1 teaspoon of lemon juice.

Make paste with 2 teaspoons of lemon juice and the rest of the spices. Rub the paste onto the lamb.

Roast lamb in 400° F oven for 30 minutes. Drain off fat and add vermouth and onions.

Reduce heat to 325° F and cook for an additional 1¾–2 hours. Baste leg of lamb frequently.

When internal temperature is 145° F, remove from oven and let rest 3 minutes before serving.

Nutrition	Calories	292	Fat	20g	Carbs	2g	Protein	24g	Sodium	157mg	Phosphorus	101mg	Potassium	53mg

102. Eggplant And Red Pepper Soup

Preparation Time: 20 minutes | Cooking Time: 40 minutes | Servings: 6

Ingredients:

- Sweet onion – 1 small, cut into quarters
- Small red bell peppers – 2, halved
- Cubed eggplant – 2 cups
- Garlic – 2 cloves, crushed
- Olive oil – 1 Tbsp.

- Chicken stock – 1 cup
- Water
- Chopped fresh basil – ¼ cup
- Ground black pepper

Directions:

Preheat the oven to 350°F. Put the onions, red peppers, eggplant, and garlic in a baking dish.

Drizzle the vegetables with the olive oil. Roast the vegetables for 30 minutes or until they are slightly charred and soft.

Cool the vegetables slightly and remove the skin from the peppers.

Puree the vegetables with a hand mixer (with the chicken stock). Transfer the soup to a medium pot and add enough water to reach the desired thickness.

Heat the soup to a simmer and add the basil. Season with pepper and serve.

Nutrition	Calories	61	Fat	2g	Carbs	9g	Protein	2g	Sodium	98mg	Phosphorus	122mg	Potassium	198mg

103. Ground Beef And Rice Soup

Preparation Time: 15 minutes | Cooking Time: 40 minutes | Servings: 4

Ingredients:

- Extra-lean ground beef – ½ pound
- Small sweet onion – ½, chopped
- Minced garlic – 1 tsp.
- Water – 2 cups
- Low-sodium beef broth – 1 cup

- Long-grain white rice – ½ cup, uncooked
- Celery stalk – 1, chopped
- Fresh green beans – ½ cup, cut into – 1-inch pieces
- Chopped fresh thyme – 1 tsp.
- Ground black pepper

Directions:

Sauté the ground beef in a saucepan for 6 minutes or until the beef is completely browned. Drain off the excess fat and add the onion and garlic to the saucepan.

Sauté the vegetables for about 3 minutes, or until they are softened. Add the celery, rice, beef broth, and water.

Bring the soup to a boil, reduce the heat to low and simmer for 30 minutes or until the rice is tender.

Add the green beans and thyme and simmer for 3 minutes. Remove the soup from the heat and season with pepper.

Nutrition	Calories	154	Fat	7g	Carbs	14g	Protein	9g	Sodium	133mg	Phosphorus	201mg	Potassium	217mg

104. Persian Chicken

Preparation Time: 10 minutes | Cooking Time: 20 minutes | Servings: 5

Ingredients:

- Sweet onion – ½, chopped
- Lemon juice – ¼ cup
- Dried oregano – 1 Tbsp.
- Minced garlic – 1 tsp.

- Sweet paprika – 1 tsp.
- Ground cumin – ½ tsp.
- Olive oil – ½ cup
- Boneless, skinless chicken thighs – 5

Directions:

Put the cumin, paprika, garlic, oregano, lemon juice, and onion in a food processor and pulse to mix the Ingredients.

Keep the motor running and add the olive oil until the mixture is smooth.

Place the chicken thighs in a large sealable freezer bag and pour the marinade into the bag.

Seal the bag and place in the refrigerator, turning the bag twice, for 2 hours.

Remove the thighs from the marinade and discard the extra marinade.

Preheat the barbecue to medium.

Grill the chicken for about 20 minutes, turning once, until it reaches 165°F.

Nutrition	Calories	321	Fat	21g	Carbs	3g	Protein	22g	Sodium	86mg	Phosphorus	71mg	Potassium	137mg

105. Eggplant and Red Pepper Soup
***Preparation Time:** 20 minutes | **Cooking Time:** 40 minutes | **Servings:** 6*

Ingredients:

- Sweet onion – 1 small, cut into quarters
- Small red bell peppers – 2, halved
- Cubed eggplant – 2 cups
- Garlic – 2 cloves, crushed
- Olive oil – 1 Tbsp.
- Chicken stock – 1 cup
- Water
- Chopped fresh basil – ¼ cup
- Ground black pepper

Directions:

Preheat the oven to 350°F. Put the onions, red peppers, eggplant, and garlic in a baking dish.

Drizzle the vegetables with the olive oil.

Roast the vegetables for 30 minutes or until they are slightly charred and soft.

Cool the vegetables slightly and remove the skin from the peppers.

Puree the vegetables with a hand mixer (with the chicken stock).

Transfer the soup to a medium pot and add enough water to reach the desired thickness.

Heat the soup to a simmer and add the basil. Season with pepper and serve.

Nutrition	Calories	61	Fat	2g	Carbs	9g	Protein	2g	Sodium	98mg	Phosphorus	110mg	Potassium	144mg

106. Seafood Casserole
***Preparation Time:** 20 minutes | **Cooking Time:** 45 minutes | **Servings:** 6*

Ingredients:

- Eggplant – 2 cups, peeled and diced into 1-inch pieces
- Butter, for greasing the baking dish
- Olive oil – 1 tbsp.
- Sweet onion – ½, chopped
- Minced garlic - 1 tsp.
- Celery stalk – 1, chopped
- Red bell pepper – ½, boiled and chopped
- Freshly squeezed lemon juice – 3 Tbsps.
- Hot sauce – 1 tsp.
- Creole seasoning mix – ¼ tsp.
- White rice – ½ cup, uncooked
- Egg – 1 large
- Cooked shrimp – 4 ounces
- Queen crab meat – 6 ounces

Directions:

Preheat the oven to 350°F. Boil the eggplant in a saucepan for 5 minutes. Drain and set aside.

Grease a 9-by-13-inch baking dish with butter and set aside.

Heat the olive oil in a large skillet over medium heat.

Sauté the garlic, onion, celery, and bell pepper for 4 minutes or until tender.

Add the sautéed vegetables to the eggplant, along with the lemon juice, hot sauce, seasoning, rice, and egg.

Stir to combine. Fold in the shrimp and crab meat.

Spoon the casserole mixture into the casserole dish, patting down the top.

Bake for 25 to 30 minutes or until casserole is heated through and rice is tender. Serve warm.

Nutrition	Calories	118	Fat	4g	Carbs	9g	Protein	12g	Sodium	235mg	Phosphorus	102mg	Potassium	197mg

107. Ground Beef and Rice Soup

Preparation Time: 15 minutes | Cooking Time: 40 minutes | Servings: 6

Ingredients:

- Extra-lean ground beef – ½ pound
- Small sweet onion – ½, chopped
- Minced garlic – 1 tsp
- Water – 2 cups
- Low-sodium beef broth – 1 cup
- Long-grain white rice – ½ cup, uncooked
- Celery stalk – 1, chopped
- Fresh green beans – ½ cup, cut into – 1-inch pieces
- Chopped fresh thyme – 1 tsp
- Ground black pepper

Directions:

Sauté the ground beef in a saucepan for 6 minutes or until the beef is completely browned.

Drain off the excess fat and add the onion and garlic to the saucepan.

Sauté the vegetables for about 3 minutes, or until they are softened.

Add the celery, rice, beef broth, and water.

Bring the soup to a boil, reduce the heat to low and simmer for 30 minutes or until the rice is tender.

Add the green beans and thyme and simmer for 3 minutes.

Remove the soup from the heat and season with pepper.

Nutrition	Calories	154	Fat	7g	Carbs	14g	Protein	9g	Sodium	178mg	Phosphorus	76mg	Potassium	179mg

108. Couscous Burgers

Preparation Time: 20 minutes | Cooking Time: 10 minutes | Servings: 4

Ingredients:

- Canned chickpeas – ½ cup, rinsed and drained
- Chopped fresh cilantro – 2 Tbsps
- Chopped fresh parsley
- Lemon juice - 1 Tbsp
- Lemon zest – 2 tsps.
- Minced garlic – 1 tsp.
- Cooked couscous – 2 ½ cups
- Eggs – 2 lightly beaten
- Olive oil – 2 Tbsps

Directions:

Put the cilantro, chickpeas, parsley, lemon juice, lemon zest, and garlic in a food processor and pulse until a paste form.

Transfer the chickpea mixture to a bowl and add the eggs and couscous. Mix well.

Chill the mixture in the refrigerator for 1 hour. Form the couscous mixture into 4 patties.

Heat olive oil in a skillet. Place the patties in the skillet, 2 at a time, gently pressing them down with a spatula.

Cook for 5 minutes or until golden and flip the patties over. Cook the other side for 5 minutes and transfer the cooked burgers to a plate covered with a paper towel.

Repeat with the remaining 2 burgers.

Nutrition	Calories	242	Fat	10g	Carbs	29g	Protein	9g	Sodium	43mg	Phosphorus	108mg	Potassium	167mg

109. Baked Flounder

Preparation Time: 20 minutes | Cooking Time: 5 minutes | Servings: 4

Ingredients:

- Homemade mayonnaise – ¼ cup
- Juice of 1 lime
- Zest of 1 lime
- Chopped fresh cilantro – ½ cup
- Flounder fillets – 4 (3-ounce)
- Ground black pepper

Directions:

Preheat the oven to 400°F. In a bowl, stir together the cilantro, lime juice, lime zest, and mayonnaise.

Place 4 pieces of foil, about 8 by 8 inches square, on a clean work surface.

Place a flounder fillet in the center of each square. Top the fillets evenly with the mayonnaise mixture.

Season the flounder with pepper.

Fold the sides of the foil over the fish, creating a snug packet, and place the foil packets on a baking sheet.

Bake the fish for 4 to 5 minutes. Unfold the packets and serve.

Nutrition	Calories	92	Fat	4g	Carbs	2g	Protein	12g	Sodium	267mg	Phosphorus	209mg	Potassium	137mg

110. Persian Chicken

Preparation Time: 10 minutes | Cooking Time: 20 minutes | Servings: 5

Ingredients:

- Sweet onion – ½, chopped
- Lemon juice – ¼ cup
- Dried oregano – 1 Tbsp.
- Minced garlic – 1 tsp.
- Sweet paprika – 1 tsp.
- Ground cumin – ½ tsp.
- Olive oil – ½ cup
- Boneless, skinless chicken thighs – 5

Directions:

Put the cumin, paprika, garlic, oregano, lemon juice, and onion in a food processor and pulse to mix the Ingredients.

Keep the motor running and add the olive oil until the mixture is smooth.

Place the chicken thighs in a large sealable freezer bag and pour the marinade into the bag.

Seal the bag and place in the refrigerator, turning the bag twice, for 2 hours.

Remove the thighs from the marinade and discard the extra marinade.

Preheat the barbecue to medium.

Grill the chicken for about 20 minutes, turning once, until it reaches 165°F.

Nutrition	Calories	321	Fat	21g	Carbs	3g	Protein	22g	Sodium	86mg	Phosphorus	131mg	Potassium	220mg

111. Pork Souvlaki
Preparation Time: 20 minutes | Cooking Time: 12 minutes | Servings: 8

Ingredients:

- Olive oil – 3 Tbsps.
- Lemon juice – 2 Tbsps.
- Minced garlic – 1 tsp.
- Chopped fresh oregano – 1 Tbsp.
- Ground black pepper – ¼ tsp.
- Pork leg – 1 pound, cut in 2-inch cubes

Directions:

In a bowl, stir together the lemon juice, olive oil, garlic, oregano, and pepper.

Add the pork cubes and toss to coat.

Place the bowl in the refrigerator, covered, for 2 hours to marinate.

Thread the pork chunks onto 8 wooden skewers that have been soaked in water.

Preheat the barbecue to medium-high heat.

Grill the pork skewers for about 12 minutes, turning once, until just cooked through but still juicy.

Nutrition	Calories	95	Fat	4g	Carbs	0g	Protein	13g	Sodium	29mg	Phosphorus	124mg	Potassium	230mg

112. Pork Meatloaf
Preparation Time: 10 minutes | Cooking Time: 50 minutes | Servings: 8

Ingredients:

- 95% lean ground beef – 1 pound
- Breadcrumbs – ½ cup
- Chopped sweet onion – ½ cup
- Egg – 1
- Chopped fresh basil – 2 Tbsps.
- Chopped fresh thyme -1 tsp.
- Chopped fresh parsley – 1 tsp.
- Ground black pepper – ¼ tsp.
- Brown sugar – 1 Tbsp.
- White vinegar – 1 tsp.
- Garlic powder – ¼ tsp.

Directions:

Preheat the oven to 350°F.

Mix together the breadcrumbs, beef, onion, basil, egg, thyme, parsley, and pepper until well combined.

Press the meat mixture into a 9-by-5-inch loaf pan.

In a small bowl, stir together the brown sugar, vinegar, and garlic powder.

Spread the brown sugar mixture evenly over the meat.

Bake the meatloaf for about 50 minutes or until it is cooked through.

Let the meatloaf stand for 10 minutes and then pour out any accumulated grease.

Nutrition	Calories	103	Fat	3g	Carbs	7g	Protein	11g	Sodium	87mg	Phosphorus	112mg	Potassium	190mg

113. Chicken Stew

Preparation Time: 20 minutes | Cooking Time: 50 minutes | Servings: 6

Ingredients:

- Olive oil – 1 Tbsp.
- Boneless, skinless chicken thighs – 1 pound, cut into 1-inch cubes
- Sweet onion – ½, chopped
- Minced garlic – 1 Tbsp.
- Chicken stock – 2 cups
- Water – 1 cup, plus 2 Tbsps.
- Carrot – 1, sliced
- Celery – 2 stalks, sliced
- Turnip – 1, sliced thin
- Chopped fresh thyme – 1 Tbsp.
- Chopped fresh rosemary – 1 tsp.
- Cornstarch – 2 tsps.
- Ground black pepper to taste

Directions:

Place a large saucepan on medium heat and add the olive oil.

Sauté the chicken for 6 minutes or until it is lightly browned, stirring often. Add the onion and garlic, and sauté for 3 minutes.

Add 1-cup water, chicken stock, carrot, celery, and turnip and bring the stew to a boil.

Reduce the heat to low and simmer for 30 minutes or until the chicken is cooked through and tender. Add the thyme and rosemary and simmer for 3 minutes more.

In a small bowl, stir together the 2 tbsps. Of water and the cornstarch; add the mixture to the stew.

Stir to incorporate the cornstarch mixture and cook for 3 to 4 minutes or until the stew thickens. Remove from the heat and season with pepper.

Nutrition	Calories	141	Fat	8g	Carbs	5g	Protein	9g	Sodium	214mg	Phosphorus	53mg	Potassium	192mg

114. Beef Chili

Preparation Time: 10 minutes | Cooking Time: 30 minutes | Servings: 2

Ingredients:

- Onion – 1, diced
- Red bell pepper – 1, diced
- Garlic – 2 cloves, minced
- Lean ground beef – 6 oz.
- Chili powder – 1 tsp.
- Oregano – 1 tsp.
- Extra virgin olive oil – 2 Tbsps.
- Water – 1 cup
- Brown rice -1 cup
- Fresh cilantro – 1 Tbsp. to serve

Directions:

Soak vegetables in warm water. Bring a pan of water to the boil and add rice for 20 minutes.

Meanwhile, add the oil to a pan and heat on medium-high heat.

Add the pepper, onions, and garlic and sauté for 5 minutes until soft. Remove and set aside.

Add the beef to the pan and stir until browned.

Add the vegetables back into the pan and stir. Now add the chili powder and herbs and the water, cover and turn the heat down a little to simmer for 15 minutes.

Meanwhile, drain the water from the rice, and the lid and steam while the chili is cooking.

Serve hot with the fresh cilantro sprinkled over the top.

Nutrition	Calories	459	Fat	22g	Carbs	36g	Protein	22g	Sodium	31mg	Phosphorus	329mg	Potassium	33mg

115. Delicious Fish Curry

Preparation Time: 5 minutes | Cooking Time: 10 minutes | Servings: 4

Ingredients:

- 1 tbsp vegetable oil
- 1 large onion, chopped
- 1 garlic clove, chopped
- 400g can tomato
- 200ml vegetable stock
- Rice or naan bread

Directions:

Heat the oil in a deep pan and gently fry the onion and garlic for about 5 mins until soft.

Add the curry paste and stir-fry for 1-2 mins, then tip in the tomatoes and stock.

Bring to a simmer, and then add the fish. Gently cook for 4-5 mins until the fish flakes easily.

Serve immediately with rice or naan

Nutrition	Calories	191	Fat	5g	Carbs	9g	Protein	30g	Sodium	154mg	Phosphorus	159mg	Potassium	147mg

116. Steak Burgers/Sandwich

Preparation Time: 10 minutes | Cooking Time: 8-10 minutes | Servings: 4

Ingredients:

- 1 tablespoon lemon juice
- 1 tablespoon Italian seasoning
- 1 teaspoon black pepper
- 4 flank steaks (around 4 oz. each)
- 1 medium red onion, sliced
- 1 tablespoon vegetable oil
- 4 sandwich/burger buns

Directions:

Season steaks with lemon juice, Italian seasoning, and black pepper.

Take a medium saucepan or skillet, add oil. Heat over medium heat.

Add steaks and stir-cook for 5-6 minutes until evenly brown. Set aside.

Add onion and stir-cook for 2-3 minutes until it becomes translucent and softened.

Slice burger buns into half and place 1 steak piece over.

Add onion mixture on top. Add another bun piece on top and serve fresh.

Nutrition	Calories	349	Fat	12g	Carbs	9g	Protein	36g	Sodium	287mg	Phosphorus	321mg	Potassium	247mg

117. Hearty Meatloaf

Preparation Time: 10 minutes | Cooking Time: 50 minutes | Servings: 8

Ingredients:

- 1 large egg
- 2 tablespoons chopped fresh basil
- 1 teaspoon chopped fresh thyme
- 1 teaspoon chopped fresh parsley
- ¼ teaspoon black pepper (ground)
- 1 pound 95% lean ground beef
- ½ cup breadcrumbs
- ½ cup chopped sweet onion
- 1 teaspoon white vinegar
- ¼ teaspoon garlic powder
  1 tablespoon brown sugar

Directions:

Preheat an oven to 350⁰F.Grease a loaf pan (9X5-inch) with some cooking spray.

In a mixing bowl, add beef, breadcrumbs, onion, egg, basil, thyme, parsley, and black pepper.

Combine to mix well with each other.

Add the mixture in the pan.

Take another mixing bowl; add brown sugar, vinegar, and garlic powder. Combine to mix well with each other.

Add brown sugar mixture over the meat mixture. Bake for about 50 minutes until golden brown. Serve warm.

Nutrition	Calories	118	Fat	3g	Carbs	8g	Protein	12g	Sodium	106mg	Phosphorus	129mg	Potassium	203mg

118. Smoked Creamy Fish Fat Bombs
Preparation Time: 10 minutes | Cooking Time: 35 minutes | Servings: 2

Ingredients:

- 1/4 cup of mayonnaise
- 1 cup cream cheese
- 1 Tbsp of mustard
- 1 filet smoked fish, boneless, crumbled
- 2 Tbsp grated cheese
- 1 tsp fresh parsley, chopped

Directions:

Combine all Ingredients and beat in a food processor.

Make 6 balls and place them on a lined pan with parchment paper.

Refrigerate for 3 hours.

Serve cold.

Nutrition	Calories	221	Fat	15g	Carbs	2g	Protein	20g	Sodium	123mg	Phosphorus	102mg	Potassium	233mg

119. Steamed Bream with Fennel
Preparation Time: 10 minutes | Cooking Time: 20 minutes | Servings: 4

Ingredients:

- 2 Tbsp of olive oil
- 4 Tbsp of water
- 2 large spring onion, sliced
- 1 sprig of fresh rosemary, only the leaves, chopped
- 1 clove of garlic, crushed
- 4 fillets of sea bream (about 1 1/2 lbs.)
- Juice of 1 lemon
- 4 Tbsp of fresh fennel
- Salt and ground pepper

Directions:

Heat the olive oil in a large skillet. Add the spring onions, cover and cook for 7 - 8 minutes on medium heat.

Next, add the garlic, water rosemary, salt, pepper, stir and cook for 2 - 3 minutes.

In a large pot heat water and set a steamer with the fish.

Cover the pot and steam the fish for 8 minutes.

Remove fish on a plate, and cover with the spring onion sauce. Sprinkle with chopped fennel, and drizzle with fresh lemon juice.

Nutrition	Calories	281	Fat	12g	Carbs	5g	Protein	38g	Sodium	104mg	Phosphorus	74mg	Potassium	114mg

120. Egg and Fish Fry

Preparation Time: 15 minutes | Cooking Time: 15 minutes | Servings: 3

Ingredients:

- 1 lbs. Fish fillet-skinless and boneless (Tilapia, Catfish or any white fish)
- 1/2 Lime juice
- Sea salt
- 1 green onion
- 1/2-inch ginger

- 3 cloves garlic
- 1/2 cup cilantro
- 2 green chilies
- 1 egg
- 1 cup ground almonds
- Oil for frying

Directions:

Cut the fish fillet into pieces, rinse and pat dry. Put the fish fillets in a plastic bag and marinate with lime juice and the salt.

Make a fine paste with onion, ginger, garlic, green chilies and cilantro, using a food processor, Vitamix or blender.

Add the paste to the marinade and shake to combine well. Remove the fish pieces only, and discard the excess marinate.

Whisk the egg with 2-3 tbsp of water to have a smooth consistency.

Spread the ground almonds on a flat surface.

Dip the fish piece in the egg mixture, and then roll into ground almonds.

Heat the oil in deep frying skillet. Fry the fish fillets until get a nice golden-brown color.

Remove from the skillet and place on a paper towel to absorb the excess oil. Serve hot.

Nutrition	Calories	381	Fat	19g	Carbs	9g	Protein	44g	Sodium	178mg	Phosphorus	259mg	Potassium	144mg

121. Tuna Salad with Avocado, Sesame and Mint

Preparation Time: 15 minutes | Cooking Time: 15 minutes | Servings: 6

Ingredients:

- 1 cucumber, sliced
- 1 pepper green, hot
- 1 avocado
- 1 zucchini, sliced
- Juice and zest of 2 limes

- 1/4 cup of olive oil
- Salt and ground pepper
- 1 lbs. of tuna, fresh
- 2 Tbsp of sesame seeds
- 2 - 3 Tbsp of fresh mint, finely chopped

Directions:

Cut the cucumber in the middle and then at 4 slices.

Clean and slice the pepper, avocado, zucchini and place in a large bowl.

Pour with fresh lime juice and drizzle with olive oil.

Cut the tuna fish into large pieces, and season with the salt and pepper.

Heat some oil in a skillet at high heat, and fry tuna slices for 2-3 minutes.

Remove the tuna from the pan and transfer in a salad bowl; gently stir.

Sprinkle with sesame seeds and fresh mint and serve immediately.

Nutrition	Calories	331	Fat	23g	Carbs	9g	Protein	24g	Sodium	235mg	Phosphorus	255mg	Potassium	147mg

122. Almond Breaded Crayfish with Herbs

Preparation Time: 20 minutes | Cooking Time: 5 minutes | Servings: 6

Ingredients:

- 1 cup of grated almonds
- The zest of one orange
- 1 bunch of parsley
- 3/4 cup of olive oil

- Salt and ground pepper
- 30 crayfish, cleaned
- 2 lemons For serving

Directions:

Place grated almonds, orange zest, parsley, 3 tablespoons of oil, and the salt and ground pepper in a blender.

Pour the almond mixture to the deep plate and roll on each crayfish.

Heat the oil in a large skillet over high heat.

Cook crayfish for 5 minutes turning 2 - 3 times.

Serve hot with lemon wedges.

Nutrition	Calories	489	Fat	9g	Carbs	9g	Protein	12g	Sodium	79mg	Phosphorus	106mg	Potassium	213mg

123. Aromatic Cuttlefish with Spinach

Preparation Time: 10 minutes | Cooking Time: 1 hour | Servings: 6

Ingredients:

- 2 lbs. of cuttlefish
- 3/4 cup of olive oil
- 3 cups of water
- 3/4 cup of fresh anis

- 1 lbs. of fresh spinach
- 1 small tomato, grated
- Juice of 1 large lemon
- Salt and pepper to taste

Directions:

Clean and rinse thoroughly the cuttlefish. Heat the oil in a large skillet and sauté the onion for 1-2 minutes over medium heat.

Add the cuttlefish and cook until get the color.

Pour 3 cups of water, close the pot lid and simmer for at least 40-45 minutes.

Add the spinach, anis, grated tomato, salt and ground pepper.

Close the lid again and continue cooking at low temperature until the herbs soften.

Pour in the lemon juice and mix well. Serve warm.

Nutrition	Calories	378	Fat	28g	Carbs	5.5g	Protein	27g	Sodium	109mg	Phosphorus	253mg	Potassium	292mg

124. Baked Shrimp Saganaki with Feta

Preparation Time: 10 minutes | Cooking Time: 15 minutes | Servings: 6

Ingredients:

- 1 cup of olive oil
- 1 large grated tomato
- 1 green onion, sliced
- 2 lbs. of large shrimp

- 2 cups of feta cheese, crumbled
- Salt and ground pepper to taste
- 1 cup of fresh parsley, chopped For serving

Directions:

Preheat the oven to 350° F.

In a large skillet heat the olive oil and cook the green onion and tomato.

Season with the salt and pepper and cook for 2 minutes. Add shrimp and stir for 2 minutes.

Finally, sprinkle feta cheese evenly over the shrimp. Place in oven and bake for 6 -8 minutes.

Serve hot with chopped parsley.

Nutrition	Calories	516	Fat	48g	Carbs	5g	Protein	28g	Sodium	174mg	Phosphorus	173mg	Potassium	192mg

125. Breaded Catfish Fillets

Preparation Time: 15 minutes | Cooking Time: 10 minutes | Servings: 4

Ingredients:

- 1/2 cup ground almonds
- 1/2 tsp sea salt
- 1/8 tsp freshly-ground black pepper
- 1/2 tsp of garlic powder
- 1 1/2 lbs. catfish fillets
- 2 eggs, beaten
- Olive oil for frying

Directions:

In a bowl, combine ground almonds, salt, garlic powder and pepper.

Dip catfish fillets in beaten egg, then coat well with the almond mixture.

Heat the oil in a large skillet and cook breaded fish for 4 minutes from each side over medium heat.

Turn only once during cooking. Serve hot.

Nutrition	Calories	410	Fat	29g	Carbs	5.5g	Protein	32g	Sodium	103mg	Phosphorus	103mg	Potassium	171mg

126. Calamari and Shrimp Stew

Preparation Time: 10 minutes | Cooking Time: 15 minutes | Servings: 4

Ingredients:

- 3 Tbsp olive oil
- 1 green onion, finely chopped
- 3 cloves garlic, minced
- 3 lbs. shrimp cleaned and deveined
- 1 lbs. of calamari rings, frozen
- 1/4 can of white wine
- 1/2 can fresh parsley, finely chopped
- 1 grated tomato
- Salt and freshly ground black pepper

Directions:

Add the shrimps and calamari rings.

Stir and cook for about 3 - 4 minutes over medium heat.

Add the wine, parsley and grated tomato.

Season the salt and pepper to taste.

Cover and cook for 4 -5 minutes.

Serve hot with chopped parsley.

Nutrition	Calories	184	Fat	7g	Carbs	4.5g	Protein	24g	Sodium	87mg	Phosphorus	201mg	Potassium	192mg

127. Catalonian Shrimp Stew

Preparation Time: 5 minutes | Cooking Time: 15 minutes | Servings: 4

Ingredients:

- 1/2 cup olive oil
- 1 1/2 lbs. shrimp, peeled and devei ned
- 36 garlic cloves, minced
- 1/4 cup fresh lemon juice

- 1 tsp red pepper flakes (to taste)
- 4 Tbsp of fresh parsley, chopped
- Salt and fresh ground pepper

Directions:

In a large skillet heat the on high heat.

Add shrimp and garlic and sauté for about 2-3 minutes.

Add the lemon juice, pepper flakes, and salt and pepper to taste. Serve hot with chopped parsley.

Nutrition	Calories	403	Fat	29g	Carbs	50g	Protein	25.9g	Sodium	73mg	Phosphorus	103mg	Potassium	98mg

128. Cuttlefish with Green Olives and Fennel

Preparation Time: 10 minutes | Cooking Time: 20 minutes | Servings: 6

Ingredients:

- 2/3 glass of olive oil
- 2 green onions, finely chopped
- 2 cloves of garlic, minced
- 2 lbs. of cuttlefish cleaned (or squid, calamari if cuttlefish is unavailable or difficult to find. Adjust cooking times accordingly)

- 2/3 glass of red wine
- 1/2 cup of water
- 11 oz of green olives, pitted
- 1 bunch of fresh fennels, chopped
- Salt and ground black pepper

Directions:

Wash the cuttlefish very well and cut into thick pieces.

Heat the oil in a large skillet over medium-high heat.

Add green onion, garlic and cuttlefish; sauté for 2 - 3 minutes.

Pour the wine and water and stir for 5 -6 minutes over low heat.

In a meantime, in a separate pot, boil the fennel for 3 minutes.

Strain the fennel and add along with olives in a skillet with cuttlefish; stir.

Season with the salt and pepper, cover and cook for 2 - 3 minutes. Serve hot.

Nutrition	Calories	433	Fat	30g	Carbs	9g	Protein	26g	Sodium	122mg	Phosphorus	144mg	Potassium	187mg

129. Delicious Shrimp with Broccoli

Preparation Time: 10 minutes | Cooking Time: 20 minutes | Servings: 4

Ingredients:

- 2 Tbsp sesame oil
- 2 large cloves garlic, minced
- 1 cup water
- 2 Tbsp coconut aminos (from coconut sap)

- 2 tsp fresh ginger root, grated
- 2 cups fresh broccoli florets
- 1 1/2 lbs. shrimp, peeled and deveined
- Lemon wedges For serving

Directions:

Heat the oil in a large skillet or wok over medium-high heat.

Cook the garlic for about 3 - 4 minutes.

Reduce the heat to low; add water, coconut aminos, and ginger.

Bring the mixture to a boil, and shrimp; cook and stir until the shrimp turn pink, about 3 to 4 minutes.

Add broccoli and cook for 10 minutes. Serve hot with lemon wedges.

Nutrition	Calories	220	Fat	10g	Carbs	9g	Protein	27g	Sodium	144mg	Phosphorus	153mg	Potassium	172mg

130. Fried Mussels with Mustard and Lemon
Preparation Time: 10 minutes | Cooking Time: 10 minutes | Servings: 6

Ingredients:

- 1/4 cup garlic-infused olive oil
- 2 spring onions, finely chopped
- 1 small green pepper, chopped
- 2 cherry tomatoes
- 1 tsp oregano
- 1 1/2 lbs. mussels with shells, freshly cleaned
- 1 cup water
- 2 Tbsp mustard (Dijon, English, ground stone)
- Freshly ground pepper to taste
- Pinch of cayenne pepper (optional)
- 2 lemons, juice, zest and slices

Directions:

Heat the oil in a large frying skillet over high heat.

Sauté fresh onion, pepper, oregano and chopped tomatoes for 2-3 minutes.

Add the mussels and water and cover. Cook for 2-3 minutes on high heat; shake the pan to open the mussels.

Combine the mustard with the lemon and pour over mussels.

Cook for 1 minute and sprinkle some black pepper and cayenne pepper if used. Serve with lemon juice and lemon juice.

Nutrition	Calories	301	Fat	19g	Carbs	9.5g	Protein	22g	Sodium	200mg	Phosphorus	203mg	Potassium	212mg

131. Fried Wine Octopus Patties
Preparation Time: 10 minutes | Cooking Time: 10 minutes | Servings: 6

Ingredients:

- 2 lbs. octopus fresh or frozen, cleaned and cut in small cubes
- 1 cup of ground almond
- 1 cup of red wine
- 2 spring onions finely chopped
- 1 Tbsp of oregano
- Salt and ground black pepper
- 1 cup of olive oil

Directions:

In a deep bowl, combine the octopus cubes, ground almond, red wine, spring onions, oregano, and the salt and the pepper.

Knead until combined well.

Form the mixture into balls or patties. Heat the oil in a large and deep fry pan.

Fry octopus patties until get a golden color. Transfer the octopus patties on a platter lined with kitchen paper towel and serve warm.

Nutrition	Calories	526	Fat	49.5g	Carbs	8g	Protein	28g	Sodium	144mg	Phosphorus	273mg	Potassium	292mg

132. Grilled King Prawns with Parsley Sauce

Preparation Time: 10 minutes | Cooking Time: 15 minutes | Servings: 4

Ingredients:

- 40 king prawns, heads off and unpeeled
- 1/4 cup olive oil
- 2 green onions (scallions), finely chopped
- 2 Tbsp of fresh parsley, finely chopped
- 3 Tbsp water
- Salt and pepper to taste

Directions:

Cut prawns in half so that the meat is exposed in the shell.

In a large skillet heat the olive oil and sauté the green onion for 2 - 3 minutes or until softened.

Add chopped parsley, water, salt and pepper: stir for 2 minutes and remove from the heat.

Preheat your grill (pellet, gas, charcoal) to HIGH according to manufacturer Instructions.

Brush prawns with onion - parsley mixture, and grill for 3 - 4 each side. Serve hot.

Nutrition	Calories	209	Fat	4g	Carbs	3g	Protein	38g	Sodium	79mg	Phosphorus	93mg	Potassium	102mg

133. Cajun Lime Grilled Shrimp

Preparation Time: 10 minutes **Cooking Time**: 15 minutes **Servings**: 6

Ingredients:

- 3 Tbsp Cajun seasoning
- 2 lime, juiced
- 2 Tbsp olive oil
- 1 lbs. peeled and deveined medium shrimp (30-40 per pound)

Directions:

Mix together the Cajun seasoning, lime juice, and olive oil in a resalable plastic bag.

Add the shrimp, coat with the marinade, squeeze out excess air, and seal the bag.

Marinate in the refrigerator for 20 minutes.

Preheat your grill (pellet, gas, charcoal) to HIGH according to manufacturer Instructions.

Remove the shrimp from the marinade and shake off excess. Discard the remaining marinade.

Grill shrimp until they are bright pink on the outside and the meat is no longer transparent in the center, about 2 minutes per side. Serve hot.

Nutrition	Calories	318	Fat	17g	Carbs	8.7g	Protein	32g	Sodium	103mg	Phosphorus	93mg	Potassium	172mg

134. Iberian Shrimp Fritters

Preparation Time: 10 minutes | Cooking Time: 5 minutes | Servings: 4

Ingredients:

- 1 green onion, finely diced
- 1 lbs. raw shrimp, peeled, deveined, and finely chopped
- 1 cup almond flour
- 2 Tbsp fresh parsley (chopped)
- 1 tsp baking powder
- 1 tsp hot paprika
- Salt and freshly ground black pepper, to taste
- 1/4 cup olive oil
- Lemon wedges, for serving

Directions:

In a large and deep bowl, combine green onions, shrimp, almond flour, parsley, baking powder, paprika, and pinch of the salt and pepper.

Form mixture in patties/balls/fritters. Heat the oil in a large skillet over high heat.

Fry shrimp fritters for about 5 minutes in total turning once or twice.

Using a spatula, transfer fritters to plate lined with kitchen paper towels to drain.

Serve immediately with lemon wedges.

Nutrition	Calories	271	Fat	22g	Carbs	3.5g	Protein	16g	Sodium	77mg	Phosphorus	73mg	Potassium	92mg

135. Mussels with Herbed Butter on Grill
Preparation Time: 15 minutes | Cooking Time: 10 minutes | Servings: 4

Ingredients:

- 1/2 cup of butter unsalted, softened
- 2 Tbsp fresh parsley, chopped
- 1 Tbsp of fresh dill
- 2 Tbsp of spring/green onions finely chopped
- 2 tsp lemon juice
- Salt and freshly ground pepper
- 2 lbs. of fresh mussels
- Lemon For serving

Directions:

In a bowl, combine butter, softened at room temperature, parsley, dill, spring onions and lemon juice.

Season with the salt and pepper to taste.

Preheat your grill (pellet, gas, charcoal) to HIGH according to manufacturer Instructions.

Grill mussels for 8 - 10 minutes or until shells open.

Remove mussels on serving plate, pour with herbed butter.

Serve with lemon.

Nutrition	Calories	401	Fat	28g	Carbs	8g	Protein	28g	Sodium	104mg	Phosphorus	142mg	Potassium	92mg

136. Mussels with Saffron
Preparation Time: 5 minutes | Cooking Time: 8 minutes | Servings: 4

Ingredients:

- 2 lbs. of mussels, cleaned
- 1 onion, finely chopped
- 4 Tbsp heavy cream
- 1/2 cup of dry white wine
- Pepper to taste
- 1 pinch of saffron
- 2 Tbsp of fresh parsley, finely chopped

Directions:

In a large pot, boil the mussels with white wine, chopped onion and ground black pepper.

In a separate saucepot, boil the cream with a pinch of saffron for 2 minutes.

Drain the mussels and combine with the cream and saffron.

Serve immediately with parsley.

Nutrition	Calories	259	Fat	8g	Carbs	9g	Protein	28g	Sodium	106mg	Phosphorus	109mg	Potassium	142mg

137. Hearty Meatballs

Preparation Time: 10 minutes | Cooking Time: 20 minutes | Servings: 6

Ingredients:

- For Meatball:
- 1 tablespoon lemon juice
- ¼ teaspoon dry mustard
- ¾ teaspoon onion powder
- 1 teaspoon Italian seasoning
- 1 teaspoon poultry seasoning, unsalted
- 1 teaspoon black pepper
- 1-pound lean ground beef or turkey
- ¼ cup onion, finely chopped
- 1 teaspoon granulated sugar

- 1 teaspoon Tabasco sauce
- For Sauce:
- 1 teaspoon onion powder
- 2 teaspoons vinegar
- 2 teaspoons sugar
- ¼ cup of vegetable oil
- 2 tablespoons all-purpose flour
- 1 teaspoon Tabasco sauce
- 2-3 cups water

Directions:

Preheat an oven to 425⁰F. Grease a baking dish with some cooking spray.

In a mixing bowl, add all meatball ingredients. Combine to mix well with each other. Prepare meatballs from it and bake in a baking dish for 20 minutes until evenly brown.

Take a medium saucepan or skillet, add oil. Heat over medium heat.

Add flour, vinegar, sugar, onion powder, mild sauce, and water; stir-cook until sauce thickens. Serve meatballs with sauce on top.

Nutrition	Calories	176	Fat	11g	Carbs	6g	Protein	14g	Sodium	61mg	Phosphorus	93mg	Potassium	152mg

138. Broiled Lamb Chops

Preparation Time: 10 minutes | Cooking Time: 2 hours and 10 minutes | Servings: 6

Ingredients:

- 4 to 6 lamb loin chops
- 10 to 12 sprigs of fresh rosemary
- Four large garlic cloves halved

- 3 tablespoons of good olive oil
- 2 teaspoons of sea salt (fine)
- 1/2 teaspoon of black pepper (freshly ground)

Directions:

Set the oven to broil. Place the seasoned chops on a sheet pan that has been greased. Insert the sliced garlic cloves into the lamb chops.

Remove the leaves from the rosemary plant by placing one hand near the top of the stem and then use your fingers on the opposite hand to scrape down the entire stem from the top to the base. Or, you can simply leave the sprig whole to make it easier to remove later.

Take the fresh rosemary leaves and gently roll them between the palms of your hands to release their natural oils. Next, place a few of the freshly pressed rosemary leaves, or the just the whole spring, on top of each of the chops.

Place the lamb chops into the oven so that they are at least 8 or more inches from the heat source. Allow the lamb chops to broil until they are perfectly medium-rare, or about 8 minutes. For rare chops, about 6 minutes, or about 12 minutes for well-done chops.

When you are ready to eat the lamb chops, simply remove the garlic halves, brush the rosemary aside with your utensil, and then dig in. Large chunks of cooked garlic can be a bit overpowering to some people, while rosemary, whether fresh or dry, tends to have a woodsy texture that can make it tough to chew.

Therefore, you'll want to remove them before indulging in your lamb chops for best results.

Nutrition	Calories	169	Fat	5.9g	Carbs	8g	Protein	24g	Sodium	657mg	Phosphorus	302mg	Potassium	392mg

139. Healthy Sweet Potato Puree

Preparation Time: 10 minutes | Cooking Time: 1 hour | Servings: 8

Ingredients:

- 1/2 cup buttermilk
- 1/2 cup whole milk6 tablespoons butter

Directions:

Adjust oven rack to upper-middle position; heat to 425°F.

Place potatoes on a foil-lined pan; bake 45 to 60 minutes, until tender.

Peel when cool enough to handle.

Puree with salt and pepper in a food processor.

With motor running, gradually add milks through feeder tube, then butter.

Process until silken. (Can make up to 2 days ahead; store in an airtight container.) Reheat and serve.

Nutrition	Calories	238	Fat	9g	Carbs	3.7g	Protein	3.8g	Sodium	323mg	Phosphorus	103mg	Potassium	172mg

140. Hearty Chicken Rice Combo

Preparation Time: 10 minutes | Cooking Time: 10 minutes | Servings: 6

Ingredients:

- 12 ounces boneless, skinless chicken breast, cut into 12 strips
- Cooked white rice
- Juice of 2 limes
- 2 tablespoons brown sugar
- 1 tablespoon minced garlic
- 2 teaspoons ground cumin

Directions:

In a mixing bowl, add lime juice, brown sugar, garlic, and cumin.

Combine to mix well with each other.

Add chicken and combine well. Marinate for 1 hour in the refrigerator.

Remove chicken and thread into pre-soaked skewers.

Preheat grill over medium heat setting; grease grates with some oil.

Grill chicken 4 minutes each side until golden brown and juicy. Serve warm with cooked rice.

Nutrition	Calories	93	Fat	2g	Carbs	5g	Protein	12g	Sodium	110mg	Phosphorus	131mg	Potassium	233mg

141. Baked Eggplant Turkey

Preparation Time: 10 minutes | Cooking Time: 50 minutes | Servings: 6-8

Ingredients:

- ½ cup green pepper, chopped
- ½ cup onion, finely chopped
- 1 large eggplant
- 2 tablespoons vegetable oil
- 2 cups plain breadcrumbs
- 1 large egg, slightly beaten
- 1-pound lean ground turkey
- ½ teaspoon red pepper, optional

Directions:

Preheat an oven to 350°F. Grease a casserole dish with some cooking spray.

In boiling water, cook eggplant until fully tender. Drain and mash eggplant well.

Take a medium saucepan or skillet, add oil. Heat over medium heat.

Add onion, green pepper, and stir-cook until it becomes translucent and softened.

Add ground meat and stir-cook until evenly brown.

Mix in eggplant, egg, and breadcrumbs. Season to taste with red pepper.

Add the mixture in a casserole dish and bake for 35-45 minutes until meat is cooked to satisfaction. Serve warm.

Nutrition	Calories	263	Fat	7g	Carbs	4g	Protein	14g	Sodium	281mg	Phosphorus	162mg	Potassium	372mg

142. Italian Turkey Meatloaf

Preparation Time: 10 minutes | Cooking Time: 45 minutes | Servings: 6-8

Ingredients:

- ½ teaspoon Italian seasoning
- ¼ teaspoon black pepper
- ½ teaspoon onion powder
- ½ cup chopped onions
- 1-pound lean ground turkey

- 1 egg white
- 1 tablespoon lemon juice
- ½ cup plain breadcrumbs
- ½ cup diced green bell pepper
- ¼ cup of water

Directions:

Preheat an oven to 400°F. Grease a baking dish with some cooking spray.

In a mixing bowl, add turkey and lemon juice. Combine to mix well with each other.

Add other ingredients and combine well.

Add the mixture in a baking dish and bake for 40-45 minutes until cooked to satisfaction. Serve warm.

Nutrition	Calories	123	Fat	6g	Carbs	9g	Protein	13g	Sodium	83mg	Phosphorus	94mg	Potassium	142mg

143. Best Creamy Broccoli Soup

Preparation Time: 10 minutes | Cooking Time: 15 minutes | Servings: 5

Ingredients:

- 2 cups chicken broth
- 2 ½ cups fresh broccoli
- ¼ cup chopped onion
- 1 cup milk

- 2 tablespoons all-purpose flour
- 1 cup shredded Cheddar cheese (optional)
- ½ teaspoon dried oregano
- Salt and pepper to taste

Directions:

Bring broth to a boil. Add broccoli and onion.

Cook for five minutes, or until broccoli is tender.

In a separate bowl, slowly add milk to flour, and mix until well blended.

Nutrition	Calories	161	Fat	9.2g	Carbs	9g	Protein	10g	Sodium	481mg	Phosphorus	108mg	Potassium	142mg

Chapter 7: Snacks and Sides Recipes

144. Buffalo Cauliflower Bites with Dairy Free Ranch Dressing

Preparation Time: 15 minutes | Cooking Time: 30 minutes | Servings: 8

Ingredients:

- 4 cups of cauliflower florets
- 2 tablespoons of extra virgin olive oil
- ¼ teaspoon of salt
- ¼ teaspoon of smoked paprika
- ¼ teaspoon of garlic powder
- ½ cup of sugar free hot sauce I used Archie Moore's brand
- Dairy Free Ranch Dressing
- 1 cup organic mayonnaise

- ½ cup of Silk unsweetened coconut milk
- 1 teaspoon of garlic powder
- 1 teaspoon of onion powder
- ¼ teaspoon of pepper
- 1 tablespoon of fresh lemon juice
- ¼ cup fresh chopped parsley
- Get ingredients Powered by Chicory

Directions:

First heat oven to 400°F. Spray baking sheet with nonstick olive oil cooking spray.

Place florets in a large bowl and toss with olive oil. In a small bowl mix the salt, paprika and garlic powder together with hot sauce. Add the hot sauce into cauliflower bowl and stir well until well coated. Spread cauliflower out evenly on baking sheet and bake for 30 minutes.

Whisk ingredients together and pour into a mason jar. Cover and refrigerate until ready to serve with cauli bites.

Nutrition	Calories	123	Fat	16g	Carbs	12g	Protein	39g	Sodium	114mg	Phosphorus	107mg	Potassium	192mg

145. Baked Cream Cheese Crab Dip

Preparation Time: 5 minutes | Cooking Time: 30 minutes | Servings: 12

Ingredients:

- 8 oz. lump crab meat
- 8 oz. cream cheese softened
- ½ cup avocado mayonnaise
- 1 tablespoon lemon juice
- 1 teaspoon Worcestershire sauce

- ½ teaspoon of garlic powder
- ½ teaspoon of onion powder
- ½ teaspoon of salt
- ¼ teaspoon of dry mustard
- ¼ teaspoon of black pepper

Directions:

Add all ingredients into small baking dish and spread out evenly. Bake at 375°F for about 25 to 30 minutes. Serve with low carb crackers or vegetables.

Nutrition	Calories	167	Fat	12g	Carbs	21g	Protein	31g	Sodium	77mg	Phosphorus	1009mg	Potassium	147mg

146. Philly Cheesesteak Stuffed Mushrooms

Preparation Time: 15 minutes | Cooking Time: 15 minutes | Servings: 6

Ingredients:

- 24 oz. baby bell mushrooms
- 1 cup chopped red pepper
- 1 cup chopped onion
- 2 tablespoons butter
- 1 teaspoon salt divided

- ½ teaspoon of pepper divided
- 1 pound of beef sirloin shaved or thinly sliced against the grain
- 4 ounces of provolone cheese
- Get ingredients Powered by Chicory

Directions:

First heat oven to 350°F. Remove stems from mushrooms and place mushrooms on a greased baby sheet.

Sprinkle with ½ teaspoon of salt and ¼ teaspoon of pepper on both sides and bake for 15 minutes.

Set aside. Melt 1 tablespoon butter in a large skillet and cook pepper and onions until soft.

Then season with ½ teaspoon of salt and ¼ teaspoon of pepper.

Remove from the skillet and set aside. In the same skillet, melt the remaining tablespoon of butter and cook the meat to your preference.

Add the provolone cheese and stir until completely melted. Return back the veggies.

Add mixture into the mushrooms, top with more cheese if you like and bake for 5 minutes. Serve and enjoy.

Nutrition	Calories	435	Fat	16g	Carbs	27g	Protein	39g	Sodium	178mg	Phosphorus	203mg	Potassium	244mg

147. Greek Cookies

Preparation Time: 20 minutes | Cooking Time: 1 hour and 15 minutes | Servings: 6

Ingredients:

- ½ cup Plain yogurt
- ½ teaspoon baking powder
- 2 tablespoons Erythritol
- 1 teaspoon almond extract
- ½ teaspoon ground clove
- ½ teaspoon orange zest, grated
- 3 tablespoons walnuts, chopped
- 1 cup wheat flour
- 1 teaspoon butter, softened
- 1 tablespoon honey
- 3 tablespoons water

Directions:

In the mixing bowl mix up together Plain yogurt, baking powder, Erythritol, almond extract, ground cloves orange zest, flour, and butter.

Knead the non-sticky dough. Add olive oil if the dough is very sticky and knead it well.

Then make the log from the dough and cut it into small pieces.

Roll every piece of dough into the balls and transfer in the lined with baking paper tray.

Press the balls gently and bake for 25 minutes at 350°F.

Meanwhile, heat up together honey and water. Simmer the liquid for 1 minute and remove from the heat.

When the cookies are cooked, remove them from the oven and let them cool for 5 minutes.

Then pour the cookies with sweet honey water and sprinkle with walnuts.

Cool the cookies.

Nutrition	Calories	134	Fat	3.4g	Carbs	26.1g	Protein	4.3g	Sodium	79mg	Phosphorus	204mg	Potassium	232mg

148. Ham and Dill Pickle Bites

Preparation Time: 5 minutes | Cooking Time: 45 minutes | Servings: 15

Ingredients:

- Dill pickles
- Thin deli ham slices
- Cream cheese (or use whipped cream cheese if you prefer)

Directions:

Let the cream cheese sit for at least 30 minutes at room temperature before you make these.

Cut dill pickles lengthwise into sixths, depending on how thick the pickles are.

You need as many cut pickles spears as you have ham slices. Spread each slice of ham with a very thin layer of cream cheese.

Place a dill pickle on the edge of each ham slice. Then roll up the ham around the dill pickle, and place toothpicks where you want each piece to be cut.

Arrange on plate and serve. Enjoy.

Nutrition	Calories	217	Fat	11g	Carbs	17g	Protein	20g	Sodium	74mg	Phosphorus	103mg	Potassium	122mg

149. Easy Flavored Potatoes Mix
Preparation Time: 10 minutes | Cooking Time: 25 minutes | Servings: 2

Ingredients:

- 4 potatoes, thinly sliced
- 2 tablespoons olive oil
- 1 fennel bulb, thinly sliced
- 1 tablespoon dill, chopped
- 8 cherry tomatoes, halved
- Salt and black pepper to the taste

Directions:

Preheat your air fryer to 365 °F and add the oil. Add potato slices, fennel, dill, tomatoes, salt and pepper, toss, cover and cook for 25 minutes. Divide potato mix between plates and serve.

Nutrition	Calories	240	Fat	3g	Carbs	5g	Protein	12g	Sodium	147mg	Phosphorus	104mg	Potassium	172mg

150. Eggplant Sandwich
Preparation Time: 30 minutes | Cooking Time: 30 minutes | Servings: 2

Ingredients:

- 1 eggplant, sliced
- 2 teaspoons parsley, dried
- Salt and black pepper to the taste
- ½ cup vegan breadcrumbs
- ½ teaspoon Italian seasoning
- ½ teaspoon garlic powder
- ½ teaspoon onion powder
- 2 tablespoons almond milk
- 4 vegan bread slices
- Cooking spray
- ½ cup avocado mayo
- ¾ cup tomato sauce
- A handful basil, chopped

Directions:

Season eggplant slices with salt and pepper, leave aside for 30 minutes and then pat dry them well.

In a bowl, mix parsley with breadcrumbs, Italian seasoning, onion and garlic powder, salt and black pepper and stir.

In another bowl, mix milk with vegan mayo and also stir well.

Brush eggplant slices with mayo mix, dip them in breadcrumbs mix, place them on a lined baking sheet, spray with cooking oil, introduce baking sheet in your air fryer's basket and cook them at 400°F for 15 minutes, flipping them halfway.

Brush each bread slice with olive oil and arrange 2 of them on a working surface.

Add baked eggplant slices, spread tomato sauce and basil and top with the other bread slices, greased side down. Divide between plates and serve.

Nutrition	Calories	324	Fat	16g	Carbs	19g	Protein	12g	Sodium	104mg	Phosphorus	104mg	Potassium	201mg

151. Date and Blueberry Muffins

Preparation Time: 20 minutes | Cooking Time: 30 minutes | Servings: 12

Ingredients:

- 2 tablespoons flax meal
- 6 tablespoons water
- 1 cup almond flour
- 1 cup coconut flour
- 2 teaspoons baking soda
- 1 teaspoon sea salt
- 2 tablespoons mixed spice
- 1 cup dates, pitted
- 2 cups canned pumpkin
- 1 teaspoon lemon juice
- ¼ cup coconut oil
- 5 ounces frozen blueberries
- ¾ cup zucchini, grated
- ¾ cup chopped walnuts

Directions:

Preheat oven to 350° F. Line 12 muffin cups with paper liners.

Mix together the flax meal and water and leave for a few minutes until it becomes a gel-like consistency.

Mix almond flour, coconut flour, baking soda, sea salt and mixed spice in large bowl. Set aside.

In a food processor, pulse together the pitted dates, pumpkin and lemon juice together with the flax water and coconut oil.

Mix the pumpkin mixture into the dry ingredients. Mix well.

Gently stir in the blueberries, grated zucchini and walnuts. Divide the mixture evenly between the prepared muffin cups.

Bake for about 30 minutes. If the muffins are too gooey, after this time, leave for a few minutes longer.

Nutrition	Calories	211	Fat	12g	Carbs	23g	Protein	5g	Sodium	109mg	Phosphorus	104mg	Potassium	212mg

152. Cranberry and Lemon Cookies

Preparation Time: 20 minutes | Cooking Time: 15 minutes | Servings: 12

Ingredients:

- ½ cup coconut milk
- 1 tablespoon ground flaxseed
- 1¼ cups brown organic superfine sugar
- ½ cup unsweetened apple sauce
- ¼ cup vegetable oil
- 1 tablespoon fresh lemon juice
- 1½ teaspoons lemon zest
- 2 teaspoons vanilla extract
- 1¼ cups unbleached general-purpose flour
- 1 cup whole wheat flour
- 1 teaspoon baking soda ½ teaspoon salt
- 1 cup dried cranberries
- 1 cup chopped walnuts

Directions:

Pre-heat the oven to 350°F. Prepare 2 cookie sheets with parchment paper. Warm the coconut milk and stir in the flaxseed.

Leave to one side for it to gel. In a large bowl, stir together all of the wet ingredients with the sugar. Stir in the gelled flax seed.

In another bowl sift together the flours, baking soda and salt.

Add the flour mix to the wet ingredients a little at a time until fully combined.

When a dough has formed stir in the nuts and cranberries. Using a spoon form 2-inch round cookies on the prepared sheets.

Bake for 12 – 15 minutes until a nice golden brown.

Remove from the oven and leave to rest on the cookie sheet for about 5 minutes. Place on a cooling rack and serve

Nutrition	Calories	332	Fat	13.6g	Carbs	48.8g	Protein	4.9g	Sodium	170mg	Phosphorus	153mg	Potassium	202mg

153. No Bake Oat Cookies

Preparation Time: 30 minutes | Cooking Time: 0 minutes | Servings: 24

Ingredients:

- ½ cup plain soymilk
- 1¾ cups sugar
- ½ cup Vegan butter
- 1 teaspoon vanilla extract

- 3½ cups quick cooking oats
- ¼ cup unsweetened cocoa powder
- ½ cup smooth or crunchy peanut butter

Directions:

In a small pot combine the milk, butter, sugar, peanut butter and vanilla and cook until smooth and creamy

In a large bowl combine the oats and cocoa powder.

Pour the warm milk mixture over the oats and stir until all the ingredients have combined.

Place dollops of mixture onto a waxed paper lined cookie sheet and let cool for about half an hour.

Nutrition	Calories	171	Fat	7g	Carbs	25.5g	Protein	3.3g	Sodium	96mg	Phosphorus	97mg	Potassium	101mg

154. Chocolate Coconut Quinoa Slices

Preparation Time: 10 minutes | Cooking Time: 25 minutes | Servings: 12

Ingredients:

- ¾ cup quinoa
- ½ cup dried chopped dates
- 3 tablespoons maple syrup
- 2 tablespoons olive oil
- 2 tablespoons ground flaxseed
- ½ teaspoon almond extract

- ¼ teaspoon salt
- ½ cup chocolate protein powder
- ½ cup whole wheat flour
- ¼ cup Vegan chocolate chips
- ¼ cup shredded coconut Water

Directions::

Pre-heat the oven to 350°F. Prepare an 8 x 8 ovenproof baking dish. Grease lightly with oil.

Rinse the quinoa in cold water and leave to soak for about 10 minutes.

Drain the quinoa. Place 1 cup of water in a small saucepan bring to the boil.

Add the quinoa and simmer over a low heat for about 12 minutes. Cool.

In a food processor combine the cooked quinoa, dates, maple syrup, olive oil, flaxseed, almond extract and salt.

Process until fairly smooth. In a separate bowl stir together the chocolate protein powder, flour chocolate chips and coconut.

Fold the dry mixture into the wet mixture with a flat spatula or knife.

Press into the prepared baking dish. Even out the top.

Bake for about 25 minutes, until firm.

Cool and then slice into bars.

Store in an airtight container for about a week or freeze up to 3 months.

Nutrition	Calories	160	Fat	5g	Carbs	22.4g	Protein	9g	Sodium	38mg	Phosphorus	78mg	Potassium	92mg

155. Pineapple Raspberry Parfaits

Preparation Time: 6 minutes | Cooking Time: 0 minutes | Servings: 2

Ingredients:

- ½ pint fresh raspberries
- 1 ½ cup fresh or frozen pineapple chunks
- 2 8oz containers non-fat peach yogurt

Directions:

In a parfait glass, layer the yogurt, raspberries and pineapples alternately.

Chill inside the refrigerator and serve chilled.

Nutrition	Calories	319	Fat	1g	Carbs	60g	Protein	22g	Sodium	85mg	Phosphorus	93mg	Potassium	479mg

156. Cinnamon Apple Chips

Preparation Time: 5 minutes | Cooking Time: 3 hours | Servings: 4

Ingredients:

- 4 apples
- 1 teaspoon ground cinnamon

Directions:

Preheat the oven to 200°F. Line a baking sheet with parchment paper.

Core the apples and cut into ⅛-inch slices. Toss your cinnamon and apple slices to coat.

Spread the apples in a single layer on the prepared baking sheet.

Cook for 2 to 3 hours, until the apples are dry. They will still be soft while hot but will crisp once completely cooled. Store in an airtight container for up to four days.

Nutrition	Calories	96	Fat	0g	Carbs	26g	Protein	1g	Sodium	2mg	Phosphorus	0mg	Potassium	198mg

157. Roasted Bananas with Chocolate Yogurt Cream

Preparation Time: 10 minutes | Cooking Time: 5 minutes | Servings: 4

Ingredients:

- ½ cup whipping cream
- ½ tsp ground cinnamon
- 1 ½ cups low fat vanilla yogurt, chilled and drained
- 1 tbsp cold butter
- 1 tbsp confectioner's sugar
- 1 tbsp dark rum or lemon juice
- 2 tbsp unsweetened cocoa powder
- 3 tbsp dark brown sugar
- 4 bananas cut in strips

Directions:

Place bananas cut side up on a baking sheet coated with cooking spray. Sprinkle with brown sugar, rum and cinnamon.

Dot with butter. Roast in a 425°F preheated oven for five minutes. Turn the broiler off until the bananas are golden.

Meanwhile, beat the cocoa, cream and confectioner's sugar in a large bowl using an electric mixer.

Add the drained yogurt and fold the cream until well combined. Plate the roasted bananas and add a dollop of chocolate cream on top.

Nutrition	Calories	236	Fat	7g	Carbs	45g	Protein	7g	Sodium	91mg	Phosphorus	186mg	Potassium	722mg

158. Roasted Mint Carrots

Preparation Time: 5 minutes | Cooking Time: 20 minutes | Servings: 6

Ingredients:

- 1-pound carrots, trimmed
- 1 tablespoon extra-virgin olive oil
- Freshly ground black pepper
- ¼ cup thinly sliced mint

Directions:

Preheat the oven to 425°F.

Arrange the carrots in a single layer on a rimmed baking sheet.

Drizzle with the olive oil and shake the carrots on the sheet to coat.

Season with pepper. Roast for 20 minutes, or until tender and browned, stirring twice while cooking. Sprinkle with the mint and serve.

Nutrition	Calories	51	Fat	2g	Carbs	7g	Protein	1g	Sodium	52mg	Phosphorus	23mg	Potassium	242mg

159. Walnut Butter on Cracker

Preparation Time: 2 minutes | Cooking Time: 0 minutes | Servings: 1

Ingredients:

- 1 tablespoon walnut butter
- 2 pieces Mary's gone crackers

Directions:

Spread ½ tablespoon of walnut butter per cracker and enjoy.

Nutrition	Calories	134	Fat	14g	Carbs	5g	Protein	4g	Sodium	138mg	Phosphorus	19mg	Potassium	12mg

160. Savory Collard Chips

Preparation Time: 5 minutes | Cooking Time: 20 minutes | Servings: 4

Ingredients:

- 1 bunch collard greens
- 1 teaspoon extra-virgin olive oil
- Juice of ½ lemon
- ½ teaspoon garlic powder
- ¼ teaspoon freshly ground black pepper

Directions:

Preheat the oven to 350°F. Line a baking sheet with parchment paper.

Cut the collards into 2-by-2-inch squares and pat dry with paper towels.

In a large bowl, toss the greens with the olive oil, lemon juice, garlic powder, and pepper.

Use your hands to mix well, massaging the dressing into the greens until evenly coated.

Arrange the collards in a single layer on the baking sheet and cook for 8 minutes.

Flip the pieces and cook for an additional 8 minutes, until crisp.

Remove from the oven, let cool, and store in an airtight container in a cool location for up to three days.

Nutrition	Calories	24	Fat	1g	Carbs	3g	Protein	1g	Sodium	8mg	Phosphorus	6mg	Potassium	6mg

161. Choco-Chip Cookies with Walnuts and Oatmeal

Preparation Time: *20 minutes* | ***Cooking Time:*** *32 minutes* | ***Servings:*** *48*

Ingredients:

- ½ cup all-purpose flour
- ½ cup chopped walnuts
- ½ cup whole wheat pastry flour
- ½ tsp baking soda
- 1 cup semisweet Choco chip
- 1 large egg
- 1 large egg white
- 1 tbsp vanilla extract
- 1 tsp ground cinnamon
- 2 cups rolled oats (not quick cooking)
- 2/3 cup granulated sugar
- 2/3 cup packed light brown sugar
- 4 tbsps. cold unsalted butter, cut into pieces

Directions:

Position two racks in the middle of the oven, leaving at least a 3-inch space in between them.

Preheat oven to 350°F and grease baking sheets with cooking spray.

In medium bowl, whisk together baking soda, cinnamon, whole wheat flour, all-purpose flour and oats.

In a large bowl, with a mixer beat butter until well combined. Add brown sugar and granulated sugar, mixing continuously until creamy.

Mix in vanilla, egg white and egg and beat for a minute.

Cup by cup mix in the dry ingredients until well incorporated.

Fold in walnuts and Choco chips. Get a tablespoon full of the batter and roll with your moistened hands into a ball.

Evenly place balls into prepped baking sheets at least 2-inches apart. Pop in the oven and bake for 16 minutes.

Ten minutes into baking time, switch pans from top to bottom and bottom to top. Continue baking for 6 more minutes.

Remove from oven, cool on a wire rack.

Allow pans to cool completely before adding the next batch of cookies to be baked.

Cookies can be stored for up to 2-weeks in a tightly sealed container or longer in the ref.

Nutrition	Calories	71	Fat	3g	Carbs	12g	Protein	2g	Sodium	18mg	Phosphorus	47mg	Potassium	56mg

162. Fluffy Mock Pancakes

Preparation Time: *5 minutes* | ***Cooking Time:*** *10 minutes* | ***Servings:*** *2*

Ingredients:

- 1 egg
- 1 cup ricotta cheese
- 1 teaspoon cinnamon
- 2 tablespoons honey, add more if needed

Directions:

Using a blender, put together egg, honey, cinnamon, and ricotta cheese.

Process until all ingredients are well combined.

Pour an equal amount of the blended mixture into the pan.

Cook each pancake for 4 minutes on both sides. Serve.

Nutrition	Calories	188	Fat	14.5g	Carbs	5.5g	Protein	9g	Sodium	174mg	Phosphorus	103mg	Potassium	102mg

163. Mixes of Snack

Preparation Time: 10 minutes | Cooking Time: 1 hours and 15 minutes | Servings: 4

Ingredients:

- 6 c. margarine
- 2 tbsp. Worcestershire sauce
- 1 ½ tbsp. spice salt
- ¾ c. garlic powder
- ½ tsp. onion powder
- 3 cups Crispix

- 3 cups Cheerios
- 3 cups corn flakes
- 1 cup Kix
- 1 cup pretzels
- 1 cup broken bagel chips into 1-inch pieces

Directions:

Preheat the oven to 250°F

Melt the margarine in a large roasting pan. Stir in the seasoning. Gradually add the ingredients remaining by mixing so that the coating is uniform.

Cook 1 hour, stirring every 15 minutes.

Spread on paper towels to let cool. Store in a tightly closed container.

Nutrition	Calories		Fat	g	Carbs	g	Protein	g	Sodium	mg	Phosphorus	mg	Potassium	mg

Nutrition (For Serving): Calories: 200 kcal , Fat: 9g, Sodium: 3.5mg, Carbohydrates: 27g, Phosphorus: 47mg, Potassium: 110mg, Protein: 3g

164. Jalapeno Crisp

Preparation Time: 10 minutes | Cooking Time: 1 hour 15 minutes | Servings: 20

Ingredients:

- 1 cup sesame seeds
- 1 cup sunflower seeds
- 1 cup flaxseeds
- ½ cup hulled hemp seeds

- 3 tablespoons Psyllium husk
- 1 teaspoon salt
- 1 teaspoon baking powder
- 2 cups of water

Direction:

Preheat your oven to 350 °F. Take your blender and add seeds, baking powder, salt, and Psyllium husk

Blend well until a sand-like texture appears

Stir in water and mix until a batter forms

Allow the batter to rest for 10 minutes until a dough-like thick mixture forms

Pour the dough onto a cookie sheet lined with parchment paper

Spread it evenly, making sure that it has a thickness of ¼ inch thick all around

Bake for 75 minutes in your oven. Remove and cut into 20 spices

Allow them to cool for 30 minutes and enjoy!

Nutrition	Calories		Fat	g	Carbs	g	Protein	g	Sodium	mg	Phosphorus	mg	Potassium	mg

Nutrition (For Serving): Calories: 156 kcal , Fat: 13g, Sodium: 79mg, Carbohydrates: 2g, Phosphorus: 53mg, Potassium: 112mg, Protein: 5g

165. Raspberry Popsicle

Preparation Time: 2 hours | Cooking Time: 15 minutes | Servings: 4

Ingredients:

- 1 ½ cups raspberries
- 2 cups of water

Direction:

Take a pan and fill it up with water Add raspberries

Place it over medium heat and bring to water to a boil.

Reduce the heat and simmer for 15 minutes. Remove heat and pour the mix into Popsicle molds

Add a popsicle stick and let it chill for 2 hours and serve.

Nutrition	Calories	58	Fat	0.4g	Carbs	0g	Protein	1.4g	Sodium	14mg	Phosphorus	53mg	Potassium	82mg

166. Easy Fudge

Preparation Time: 15 minutes + chill time | Cooking Time: 5 minutes | Servings: 25

Ingredients:

- 1 ¾ cups of coconut butter
- 1 cup pumpkin puree
- 1 teaspoon ground cinnamon
- ¼ teaspoon ground nutmeg
- 1 tablespoon coconut oil

Direction:

Take an 8x8 inch square baking pan and line it with aluminum foil

Take a spoon and scoop out the coconut butter into a heated pan and allow the butter to melt

Keep stirring well and remove from the heat once fully melted

Add spices and pumpkin and keep straining until you have a grain-like texture

Add coconut oil and keep stirring to incorporate everything

Scoop the mixture into your baking pan and evenly distribute it

Place wax paper on top of the mixture and press gently to straighten the top

Remove the paper and discard

Allow it to chill for 1-2 hours

Once chilled, take it out and slice it up into pieces

Nutrition	Calories	120	Fat	10g	Carbs	5g	Protein	1.2g	Sodium	89mg	Phosphorus	78mg	Potassium	103mg

167. Cashew and Almond Butter

Preparation Time: 5 minutes | Cooking Time: 0 minutes | Servings: 2

Ingredients:

- 1 cup almonds, blanched
- 1/3 cup cashew nuts
- 2 tablespoons coconut oil
- Salt as needed
- ½ teaspoon cinnamon

Direction:

Preheat your oven to 350 °F. Bake almonds and cashews for 12 minutes. Let them cool

Transfer to a food processor and add remaining ingredients

Add oil and keep blending until smooth and serve.

Nutrition	Calories	205	Fat	19g	Carbs	9.5g	Protein	2.8g	Sodium	107mg	Phosphorus	79mg	Potassium	152mg

168. Celeriac Tortilla

Preparation Time: 10 minutes | Cooking Time: 25 minutes | Servings: 4

Ingredients:

- 2 oz celery root, peeled
- 1 potato, peeled
- 1 tablespoon almond flour
- ½ teaspoon salt
- 1 egg, beaten
- 1 teaspoon olive oil

Directions:

Place potato and celery root in the tray and bake for 15 minutes at 355F. The baked vegetables should be tender.

Then transfer them in the food processor. Blend until smooth.

Add salt, almond flour, and egg. Knead the soft dough.

Cut the dough into 4 pieces and make the balls.

Using the rolling pin roll up the dough balls in the shape of tortillas

Heat up olive oil in the skillet.

Add first celeriac tortilla and roast it for 1.5 minutes from each side.

Repeat the steps with remaining tortilla balls.

Store the cooked tortillas in the towel before serving.

Nutrition	Calories	101	Fat	5.8g	Carbs	10.3g	Protein	4g	Sodium	101mg	Phosphorus	77mg	Potassium	92mg

169. Caraway Mushroom Caps

Preparation Time: 8 minutes | Cooking Time: 25 minutes | Servings: 4

Ingredients:

- 1 teaspoon caraway seeds
- 3 oz Portobello mushroom caps
- 2 teaspoons butter, softened
- ¼ teaspoon salt

Directions:

Trim and wash mushrooms caps if needed.

Preheat the oven to 360°F.

Churn together butter with salt, and caraway seeds.

Fill the mushroom caps with butter mixture and transfer in the tray.

Bake Portobello caps for 10 minutes at 355°F.

Nutrition	Calories	24	Fat	2g	Carbs	1.3g	Protein	0.7g	Sodium	26mg	Phosphorus	53mg	Potassium	42mg

170. Stuffed Sweet Potato

Preparation Time: 10 minutes | Cooking Time: 20 minutes | Servings: 4

Ingredients:

- 4 sweet potatoes
- ¼ cup Cheddar cheese, shredded
- 2 teaspoons butter
- 1 tablespoon fresh parsley, chopped
- ½ teaspoon salt

Directions:

Make the lengthwise cut in every sweet potato and bake them for 10 minutes at 360°F.

After this, scoop ½ part of every sweet potato flesh. Fill the vegetables with salt, parsley, butter, and shredded cheese.

Return the sweet potatoes in the oven back and bake them for 10 minutes more at 355°F.

Nutrition	Calories	41	Fat	4.3g	Carbs	0.4g	Protein	1.8g	Sodium	24mg	Phosphorus	65mg	Potassium	98mg

171. Baked Olives

Preparation Time: 5 minutes | Cooking Time: 11 minutes | Servings: 3

Ingredients:

- 1 ½ cup olives
- 1 tablespoon olive oil
- 1 teaspoon dried oregano
- ¼ teaspoon dried thyme
- 1/3 teaspoon minced garlic
- ½ teaspoon salt

Directions:

Line the baking tray with baking paper. Arrange the olives in the tray in one layer.

Then sprinkle them with olive oil, dried oregano, dried thyme, minced garlic, and salt.

Bake olives for 11 minutes at 420°F.

Nutrition	Calories	119	Fat	12g	Carbs	4.7g	Protein	0.7g	Sodium	141mg	Phosphorus	77mg	Potassium	147mg

172. Sliced Figs Salad

Preparation Time: 10 minutes | Cooking Time: 25 minutes | Servings: 4

Ingredients:

- 1 tablespoon balsamic vinegar
- 1 teaspoon canola oil
- 2 tablespoons almonds, sliced
- 3 figs, sliced
- 2 cups fresh parsley
- 1 cup fresh arugula
- 2 oz Feta cheese, crumbled
- ½ teaspoon salt
- ½ teaspoon honey

Directions:

Make the salad dressing: mix up together balsamic vinegar, canola oil, salt, and honey.

Then put sliced almonds and figs in the big bowl.

Chop the parsley and add in the fig mixture too. After this, tear arugula.

Combine together arugula with fig mixture. Add salad dressing and shake the salad well.

Nutrition	Calories	116	Fat	6g	Carbs	13.1g	Protein	4.1g	Sodium	104mg	Phosphorus	13mg	Potassium	172mg

173. Lemon Cucumbers with Dill

Preparation Time: 5 minutes | Cooking Time: 30 minutes | Servings: 3

Ingredients:

- 3 cucumbers
- 3 tablespoons lemon juice
- ¾ teaspoon lemon zest
- 3 teaspoons dill, chopped
- 1 tablespoon olive oil
- ¾ teaspoon chili flakes

Directions:

Peel the cucumbers and chop them roughly. Place the cucumbers in the big glass jar.

Add lemon zest, lemon juice, dill, olive oil, and chili flakes.

Close the lid and shake well.

Marinate the cucumbers for 30 minutes.

Nutrition	Calories	92	Fat	5g	Carbs	12g	Protein	2.3g	Sodium	12mg	Phosphorus	78mg	Potassium	127mg

174. Honey Apple Bites

Preparation Time: 10 minutes | Cooking Time: 15 minutes | Servings: 2

Ingredients:

- 1 tablespoon honey
- ½ teaspoon ground cardamom
- 2 apples

Directions:

Cut the apples into halves and remove the seeds. Then cut the apples into 4 bites more.

Place the apple bites in the tray and sprinkle with ground cardamom and honey.

Bake apples for 15 minutes at 355°F.

Nutrition	Calories	149	Fat	0.4g	Carbs	40g	Protein	0.7g	Sodium	125mg	Phosphorus	102mg	Potassium	201mg

175. Cucumber Salad

Preparation Time: 10 minutes | Cooking Time: 15 minutes | Servings: 6

Ingredients:

- 2 cups tomatoes, chopped
- 1 cup cucumbers, chopped
- 1 red onion, chopped
- 1 cup fresh cilantro, chopped
- 1 red bell pepper, chopped
- 2 tablespoons sunflower oil
- 1 teaspoon salt

Directions:

In the bowl combine together tomatoes, cucumbers, onion, fresh cilantro, bell pepper, and salt.

Shake the salad mixture well.

Then add the sunflower oil. Stir the salad directly before serving.

Nutrition	Calories	69	Fat	5g	Carbs	6.3g	Protein	1.1g	Sodium	19mg	Phosphorus	47mg	Potassium	92mg

176. Sesame Seeds Escarole

Preparation Time: 10 minutes | Cooking Time: 25 minutes | Servings: 4

Ingredients:

- 1 head escarole
- 1 tablespoon sesame oil
- 1 teaspoon sesame seeds
- 1 teaspoon balsamic vinegar
- ¾ teaspoon ground black pepper
- ¼ cup of water

Directions:

Chop the escarole roughly. Pour water in the skillet and bring it to boil.

Add chopped escarole. Sauté it for 2 minutes over the high heat.

Then add sesame seeds, sesame oil, balsamic vinegar, and ground black pepper.

Mix up well and sauté escarole for 1 minute more or until it starts to boil again.

Nutrition	Calories	111	Fat	8g	Carbs	9.5g	Protein	3.6g	Sodium	47mg	Phosphorus	103mg	Potassium	144mg

177. Yogurt Eggplants

Preparation Time: 10 minutes | Cooking Time: 18 minutes | Servings: 4

Ingredients:

- 1 cup Plain yogurt
- 1 tablespoon butter
- 1 teaspoon ground black pepper
- 1 teaspoon salt
- 2 eggplants, chopped
- 1 tablespoon fresh dill, chopped

Directions:

Heat up butter in the skillet.

Toss eggplants in the hot butter.

Sprinkle them with salt and ground black pepper.

Roast the vegetables for 5 minutes over the medium-high heat.

Stir them from time to time.

After this, add fresh dill and Plain Yogurt. Mix up well.

Close the lid and simmer eggplants for 10 minutes more over the medium-high heat.

Nutrition	Calories	141	Fat	4.2g	Carbs	21.2g	Protein	6.4g	Sodium	71mg	Phosphorus	104mg	Potassium	172mg

178. Baked Zucchini Chips

Preparation Time: 10 minutes | Cooking Time: 1 hour 30 minutes | Servings: 4

Ingredients:

- Cooking spray
- 2 zucchinis, sliced very thinly into coins
- 1 tbsp. extra-virgin olive oil (for baked version only)
- 1 tbsp. ranch seasoning
- 1 tsp. dried oregano
- Kosher salt
- Freshly ground black pepper

Directions:

<u>For Oven</u>

Preheat oven to 225°. Grease a large baking sheet with cooking spray.

Slice zucchini into very thin rounds, using a mandolin if you have one! Pat zucchini with paper towels to draw out excess moisture.

In a large bowl, toss zucchini with oil then toss in ranch seasoning, oregano, salt, and pepper.

Place in a single layer on baking sheets.

Bake until crispy, about 1 hour 20 minutes, checking after about an hour. Let cool to room temperature before serving.

<u>For Air Fryer</u>

Grease air fryer basket lightly with cooking spray.

Slice zucchini into very thin rounds, using a mandolin if you have one!

Pat zucchini with paper towels to draw out excess moisture.

Air fry at 375°F for 6 minutes, then flip and cook for another 6 minutes.

Remove golden chips and continue cooking remaining chips until golden and crispy, 2 to 4 minutes, shaking basket every minute to allow for even crisping.

Nutrition	Calories	152	Fat	0.1g	Carbs	3.5g	Protein	0.6g	Sodium	77.4mg	Phosphorus	53mg	Potassium	102mg

179. Parmesan Crisps

Preparation Time: 10 minutes | Cooking Time: 30 minutes | Servings: 4

Ingredients:

- 2 ounces grated fresh Parmesan cheese (about 1/2 cup)
- 1/4 teaspoon freshly ground black pepper

Directions:

Preheat oven to 400°F.

Line a large baking sheet with parchment paper.

Spoon cheese by tablespoonfuls 2 inches apart on prepared baking sheet. Spread each mound to a 2-inch diameter.

Sprinkle mounds with pepper.

Bake at 400°F for 6 to 8 minutes or until crisp and golden.

Cool completely on baking sheet. Remove from baking sheet using a thin spatula.

Kids Can Help: Let kids sprinkle the grated cheese onto the baking sheets.

Nutrition	Calories	31	Fat	2g	Carbs	0.3g	Protein	3g	Sodium	108mg	Phosphorus	53mg	Potassium	101mg

180. Crispy Tomato Chips

Preparation Time: 20 minutes | Cooking Time: 8 minutes | Servings: 2

Ingredients:

- 2 large firm tomatoes, sliced thinly (about 1/16th of an inch)
- kosher salt
- cooking spray

Directions:

Lay sliced tomatoes on a cutting board. Sprinkle generously with salt, let sit for 15 minutes.

Pat the tomatoes with a paper towel to soak up the moisture.

Flip the tomatoes, re-salt and let sit for another 5 minutes.

Repeat the process with the paper towel.

Spray a flat, microwaveable plate with cooking spray (I used olive oil spray)

Arrange the tomato slices on the plate and spray them with cooking spray.

Microwave for 5 minutes on power level 7. (see note)

Remove the plate from the microwave, carefully flip the tomatoes and microwave for another minute.

Remove from the microwave, transfer the tomatoes which should be mostly dry and crisp at this point to a cooling rack.

Nutrition	Calories	32.7	Fat	1.3g	Carbs	3.6g	Protein	2.3g	Sodium	76.7mg	Phosphorus	73mg	Potassium	92mg

Chapter 8: Desserts Recipes

181. Cheesecake Bites

Preparation Time: 10 minutes | Cooking Time: 5 minutes | Servings: 16

Ingredients:

- 8 oz cream cheese
- 1/2 tsp vanilla
- 1/4 cup swerve

Directions:

Add all ingredients into the mixing bowl and blend until well combined. Place bowl into the fridge for 1 hour.

Remove bowl from the fridge. Make small balls from cheese mixture and place them on a baking dish. Serve and enjoy.

Nutrition	Calories	50	Fat	4.9g	Carbs	0.4g	Protein	1.1g	Sodium	79mg	Phosphorus	53mg	Potassium	92mg

182. Pumpkin Bites

Preparation Time: 10 minutes | Cooking Time: 5 minutes | Servings: 12

Ingredients:

- 8 oz cream cheese
- 1 tsp vanilla
- 1 tsp pumpkin pie spice
- 1/4 cup coconut flour
- 1/4 cup erythritol
- 1/2 cup pumpkin puree
- 4 oz butter

Directions:

Add all ingredients into the mixing bowl and beat using hand mixer until well combined.

Scoop mixture into the silicone ice cube tray and place it in the refrigerator until set. Serve and enjoy.

Nutrition	Calories	149	Fat	14.6g	Carbs	8.1g	Protein	2g	Sodium	214mg	Phosphorus	53mg	Potassium	72mg

183. Protein Balls

Preparation Time: 5 minutes | Cooking Time: 5 minutes | Servings: 12

Ingredients:

- 3/4 cup peanut butter
- 1 tsp cinnamon
- 3 tbsp erythritol
- 1 1/2 cup almond flour

Directions:

Add all ingredients into the mixing bowl and blend until well combined.

Place bowl into the fridge for 30 minutes.

Remove bowl from the fridge. Make small balls from mixture and place on a baking dish.

Serve and enjoy.

Nutrition	Calories	179	Fat	15g	Carbs	10.1g	Protein	7g	Sodium	152mg	Phosphorus	79mg	Potassium	102mg

184. Cashew Cheese Bites

Preparation Time: 5 minutes | Cooking Time: 5 minutes | Servings: 12

Ingredients:

- 8 oz cream cheese
- 1 tsp cinnamon
- 1 cup cashew butter

Directions:

Add all ingredients into the blender and blend until smooth.

Pour blended mixture into the mini muffin liners and place them in the refrigerator until set.

Serve and enjoy.

Nutrition	Calories	192	Fat	17.1g	Carbs	6.5g	Protein	5.2g	Sodium	79mg	Phosphorus	79mg	Potassium	72mg

185. Healthy Cinnamon Lemon Tea

Preparation Time: 5 minutes | Cooking Time: 5 minutes | Servings: 1

Ingredients:

- 1/2 tbsp fresh lemon juice
- 1 cup of water
- 1 tsp ground cinnamon

Directions:

Add water in a saucepan and bring to boil over medium heat. Add cinnamon and stir to cinnamon dissolve.

Add lemon juice and stir well and serve hot.

Nutrition	Calories	9	Fat	0.2g	Carbs	2g	Protein	0.2g	Sodium	12mg	Phosphorus	23mg	Potassium	32mg

186. Keto Mint Ginger Tea

Preparation Time: 5 minutes | Cooking Time: 5 minutes | Servings: 1

Ingredients:

- 1 1/2 tbsp fresh mint leaves
- 1 cup of water
- 1/2 tbsp fresh ginger, grated
- 1 tsp ground turmeric

Directions:

Add mint, ginger, and turmeric in boiling water. Stir to turmeric dissolved. Strain and serve.

Nutrition	Calories	19	Fat	0.3g	Carbs	0.5g	Protein	0.5g	Sodium	12mg	Phosphorus	13mg	Potassium	42mg

187. Energy Booster Sunflower Balls

Preparation Time: 10 minutes | Cooking Time: 10 minutes | Servings: 25

Ingredients:

- 1 cup sunflower seeds
- 2 oz unsweetened chocolate, melted
- 1 tbsp water
- 8 drops liquid stevia

Directions:

Add sunflower seeds in a blender and blend until finely ground.

Add water, stevia, and melted chocolate and blend until stiff dough like the mixture is form.

Make small balls from mixture and place on a baking tray. Place in refrigerator for 30 minutes. Serve and enjoy.

Nutrition	Calories	22	Fat	2.1g	Carbs	1.1g	Protein	0.9g	Sodium	44mg	Phosphorus	43mg	Potassium	72mg

188. Simple Berry Sorbet

Preparation Time: 5 minutes | Cooking Time: 5 minutes | Servings: 1

Ingredients:

- 1/2 cup fresh raspberries
- 1/2 cup fresh strawberries
- 5 drops liquid stevia
- 1 tsp fresh lemon juice

Directions:

Add all ingredients into the blender and blend until smooth. Pour into the air-tight container and place it in the freezer for 3-4 hours.

Serve chilled and enjoy.

Nutrition	Calories	55	Fat	0.8g	Carbs	12g	Protein	1.3g	Sodium	82mg	Phosphorus	74mg	Potassium	142mg

189. Chocolate Mousse

Preparation Time: 5 minutes | Cooking Time: 5 minutes | Servings: 4

Ingredients:

- 1/2 cup unsweetened cocoa powder
- 1/2 tsp vanilla
- 1 1/4 cup heavy cream
- 4 oz cream cheese
- 8 drops liquid stevia

Directions:

Add all ingredients into the blender and blend until smooth and creamy.

Pour mixture into the serving bowls and place in the refrigerator for 1-2 hours. Serve and enjoy.

Nutrition	Calories	255	Fat	24g	Carbs	6g	Protein	5.1g	Sodium	144mg	Phosphorus	93mg	Potassium	182mg

190. Keto Brownie

Preparation Time: 10 minutes | Cooking Time: 20 minutes | Servings: 4

Ingredients:

- 2 tbsp unsweetened cocoa powder
- 1/2 cup almond butter, melted
- 1 cup banana, overripe & mashed
- 1 scoop vanilla protein powder
- 1/2 tsp vanilla

Directions:

Preheat the oven to 350° F. Line baking dish with parchment paper and set aside.

Add all ingredients into the blender and blend until smooth. Pour batter into the prepared dish and bake for 20 minutes. Slice and serve.

Nutrition	Calories	81	Fat	2g	Carbs	10g	Protein	7g	Sodium	77mg	Phosphorus	43mg	Potassium	45mg

191. Smooth Coffee Mousse

Preparation Time: 5 minutes | Cooking Time: 5 minutes | Servings: 8

Ingredients:

- 1 cup heavy whipping cream
- 1/2 cup unsweetened almond milk
- 4 tbsp brewed coffee
- 15 oz cream cheese, softened
- 15 drops liquid stevia
- 1 tsp vanilla

Directions:

Add coffee and cream cheese in a blender and blend until smooth.

Add stevia, vanilla, and almond milk and blend until smooth.

Add heavy cream and blend until thickened. P

our into the serving bowls and place in refrigerator 1-2 hours and serve.

Nutrition	Calories	241	Fat	24.3g	Carbs	2g	Protein	4.4g	Sodium	177mg	Phosphorus	98mg	Potassium	241mg

192. Almond Bites

Preparation Time: 10 minutes | Cooking Time: 10 minutes | Servings: 12

Ingredients:

- 1/2 cup almond meal
- 2 tbsp coconut butter
- 4 dates, pitted and chopped
- 1/4 cup unsweetened chocolate chips
- 1 1/2 tsp vanilla

Directions:

Add dates in the food processor and process for 30 seconds.

Add remaining ingredients except chocolate chips and process until combined.

Add chocolate chips and process for 15 seconds.

Make small balls from mixture and place on a baking tray.

Place in refrigerator for 1-2 hours and serve.

Nutrition	Calories	53	Fat	3.8g	Carbs	4.2g	Protein	1.1g	Sodium	102mg	Phosphorus	47mg	Potassium	109mg

193. Chocolate Cookies

Preparation Time: 10 minutes | Cooking Time: 10 minutes | Servings: 18

Ingredients:

- 2 eggs, lightly beaten
- 3 tbsp butter
- 3 tbsp unsweetened cocoa powder
- 1 1/2 cups almond flour
- 1 tsp vanilla
- 1/4 cup Swerve
- 3 oz unsweetened chocolate, chopped
- Pinch of salt

Directions:

Add chocolate, butter, and cocoa powder into the pan and melt over medium-low heat.

Remove from heat and set aside.

Add eggs, vanilla, salt, and swerve in a bowl and blend until well combined.

Add melted chocolate mixture into the egg mixture and mix well.

Add almond flour and mix until well combined. Place in refrigerator for 1 hour.

Preheat the oven to 325 °F. Line baking tray with parchment paper and spray with cooking spray.

Scoop out batter onto a baking tray and bake for 10 minutes and serve

Nutrition	Calories	66	Fat	5g	Carbs	4.6g	Protein	2g	Sodium	73mg	Phosphorus	73mg	Potassium	72mg

194. Chocolate Muffins

Preparation Time: 10 minutes | Cooking Time: 30 minutes | Servings: 10

Ingredients:

- 2 eggs, lightly beaten
- 1/2 cup cream
- 1/2 tsp vanilla
- 1 cup almond flour
- 1 tbsp baking powder, gluten-free
- 4 tbsp Swerve
- 1/2 cup unsweetened cocoa powder
- Pinch of salt

Directions:

Preheat the oven to 375°F. Spray a muffin tray with cooking spray and set aside.

In a mixing bowl, mix together almond flour, baking powder, swerve, cocoa powder, and salt.

In a separate bowl, beat eggs with cream, and vanilla.

Pour egg mixture into the almond flour mixture and mix well.

Pour batter into the prepared muffin tray and bake in preheated oven for 30 minutes and serve.

Nutrition	Calories	101	Fat	8g	Carbs	6.7g	Protein	4.5g	Sodium	46mg	Phosphorus	47mg	Potassium	114mg

195. Sweet Raspberry Candy

Preparation Time: 5 minutes | Cooking Time: 5 minutes | Servings: 12

Ingredients:

- 1/2 cup dried raspberries
- 3 tbsp Swerve
- 1/2 cup coconut oil
- 2 oz cacao butter
- 1/2 tsp vanilla

Directions:

Add cacao butter and coconut oil in a saucepan and melt over low heat. Remove from heat.

Grind the raspberries in a food processor.

Add sweetener and ground raspberries into the melted butter and coconut oil mixture and stir well.

Pour mixture into the mini silicone candy molds and place them in the refrigerator until set.

Serve and enjoy.

Nutrition	Calories	103	Fat	11.5g	Carbs	1.1g	Protein	0.1g	Sodium	74mg	Phosphorus	43mg	Potassium	93mg

196. Instant Pot Cheesecake

Preparation Time: 10 minutes | Cooking Time: 38 minutes | Servings: 4

Ingredients:

- Graham Cracker Crust:
- 3 tablespoons sugar
- 5 tablespoons unsalted butter
- 9 large graham crackers, pulsed into crumbs
- 2 tablespoons ground pecans
- 1/4 teaspoons cinnamon
- Cheesecake Filling:

- 12 oz. cream cheese
- 2 teaspoons lemon zest
- 2 teaspoons vanilla extract
- 1 tablespoon cornstarch
- 1/2 cup + 2 tablespoons granulated sugar
- 2 large eggs + 1 egg yolk
- 1/2 cup sour cream

Directions:

Start by heating sugar with butter in the microwave for 40 seconds. Blend this melt with the cinnamon, pecan, and crumbs in a food processor.

Spread this mixture at the bottom of a baking pan. Place this crust in the freezer for 1 hour.

Meanwhile, prepare the filling by beating all of its ingredients in an electric mixer.

Spread this filling into the prepared crust evenly.

Pour 2 cups water into the Instant Pot and place the steam rack over it.

Place the baking pan over the rack and seal the lid. Select Manual mode with high pressure for 37 minutes.

Once the cooking is done, naturally release the pressure and remove the lid after 25 minutes.

Allow it to cool then remove the pie from the pan. Refrigerate for 3 hours at minimum. Slice and serve.

Nutrition	Calories	177	Fat	9g	Carbs	21g	Protein	3g	Sodium	95mg	Phosphorus	74mg	Potassium	144mg

197. Pots De Crème

Preparation Time: 10 minutes | Cooking Time: 6 minutes | Servings: 6

Ingredients:

- 1 1/2 cups heavy cream
- 1/2 cup coconut milk
- 5 large egg yolks

- 1/4 cup sugar
- 8 oz. bittersweet chocolate, melted
- Whipped cream and grated chocolate, to garnish

Directions:

Start by heating cream with milk in a saucepan to a simmer. Meanwhile, beat eggs yolks with sugar in a bowl.

Slowly pour in the hot milk mixture whiles stirring continuously. Add chocolate and mix until fully incorporated.

Divide this mixture into 6 custard cups of equal size.

Pour 1.5 cups water into the Instant Pot and place the double steam rack over it.

Place the 3 custard cups over one rack and other 3 on the top rack.

Seal the pot's lid and cook for 6 minutes on Manual mode with High pressure.

Once the cooking is done, release the pressure completely then remove the lid. Refrigerate the cups for 4 hours or more and serve.

Nutrition	Calories	204	Fat	8g	Carbs	30g	Protein	3g	Sodium	113mg	Phosphorus	102mg	Potassium	144mg

98. Ingredient Cheesecake

Preparation Time: 10 minutes | Cooking Time: 25 minutes | Servings: 4

Ingredients:

- Date and Nut Crust:
- 1 cup nuts
- 5 dates, roughly chopped
- Oatmeal Cookie Crust:
- ½ cup rolled oats
- ¼ cup pecans
- ¼ cup brown sugar
- 3 tablespoons melted butter
- Ingredient Cheesecake:
- 1 (14 ounces) can coconut milk with cream
- 1 cup yogurt
- Oil or butter, for greasing ramekins or cheesecake pan

Directions:

Start by mixing the yogurt with the milk in a bowl.

Divide this mixture into 4 four ramekins, greased with cooking oil. Place these ramekins in a baking pan.

After pouring 2 cups water into the Instant Pot, place the steam rack over it.

Cover the ramekins with aluminum foil and place the baking pan over the rack.

Seal the pot's lid and cook for 25 minutes on Manual mode with high pressure.

Once the cooking is done, release the pressure completely then remove the lid.

Allow the ramekins to cool at room temperature. Refrigerate them for 6 hours.

Garnish as desired and serve.

Nutrition	Calories	258	Fat	13g	Carbs	28g	Protein	5g	Sodium	214mg	Phosphorus	104mg	Potassium	241mg

199. Egg Leche Flan

Preparation Time: 10 minutes | Cooking Time: 12 minutes | Servings: 4

Ingredients:

- Caramel
- ½ cup white sugar
- 2 tablespoons water
- Custard
- 4 large eggs
- 1 can (14 oz.) coconut cream milk
- 1 can (12 oz.) almond milk
- 1 teaspoon pure vanilla extract or lemon zest

Directions:

Start by mixing sugar with water in a bowl then heat for 4 minutes in the microwave.

Mix well then divide this mixture into a baking dish. Now whisk eggs with milk, lemon zest, vanilla and coconut milk in a bowl.

Pour this mixture into the baking dish.

After pouring 1.5 cups of water into the Instant pot place a steam rack over it.

Place the baking dish over the rack and seal the pot's lid.

Cook for 12 minutes on Manual mode with high pressure.

Once the cooking is done, release the pressure completely then remove the pot's lid.

Allow the flan to cool down then refrigerate for 3 hours. Serve.

Nutrition	Calories	150	Fat	6g	Carbs	22g	Protein	2g	Sodium	67mg	Phosphorus	83mg	Potassium	102mg

200. Pot Chocolate Pudding Cake

*Preparation Time: 10 minutes | **Cooking Time:** 4 minutes | **Servings:** 4*

Ingredients:

- 2/3 cup chopped dark chocolate
- 1/2 cup applesauce
- 2 eggs
- 1 teaspoon vanilla
- 1/4 cup arrowroot
- 3 tablespoons cocoa powder
- powdered sugar for topping

Directions:

Start by pouring 2 cup water into the Instant pot and place trivet over it. Add chocolate to a ramekin and place it over the trivet.

Switch the Instant pot to the Sauté mode and cook until the chocolate melts.

Whisk eggs, applesauce, and vanilla in a mixing bowl.

Stir in all the dry ingredients and mix well until fully incorporated. Grease a 6-inch pan with butter and dust it with flour.

Spread the batter in the pan and place it in the Instant Pot. Seal the lid and cook for 4 minutes on Manual mode with High Pressure.

Once the cooking is done, release the pressure completely then remove the pot's lid. Allow the cake to cool then remove it from the pan. Slice and serve.

Nutrition	Calories	210	Fat	7g	Carbs	35g	Protein	2g	Sodium	58mg	Phosphorus	77mg	Potassium	87mg

201. Date & Carrot Cake

*Preparation Time: 10 minutes | **Cooking Time:** 50 minutes | **Servings:** 4*

Ingredients:

- Dry Cake Ingredients:
- 1 1/2 cups whole wheat pastry flour
- 3/4 teaspoons baking powder
- 3/4 teaspoons baking soda
- 1/2 teaspoons ground cinnamon
- 1/4 teaspoons ground cardamom
- 1/4 teaspoons ground allspice
- 1/4 teaspoons ground ginger
- Wet Cake Ingredients:
- 2 tablespoons ground flaxseed, mixed with 1/4 cup warm water
- 1/2 cup almond milk
- 1/4 cup avocado
- 1/2 teaspoons orange flower water, or substitute vanilla
- Cake Mix in Ingredients:
- 1 cup shredded carrot
- 1 cup chopped dates
- Icing Ingredients:
- 1/2 cup cashews
- 1/2 cup chopped dates
- 1/2 cup water, plus more as needed
- 1 1/2 teaspoons orange flower water

Directions:

Start by adding 1.5 cups of water into Instant Pot and place a trivet over it. Grease a pan with cooking oil, suitable to fit the Instant Pot.

Prepare the batter by mixing the dry and wet ingredients separately.

Now mix the two mixtures in a large bowl. Spread this batter in the prepared pan then cover it with aluminum foil.

Place the pan in the Instant Pot and seal its lid. Cook for 50 minutes on Manual mode with high pressure.

Meanwhile prepare the icing by cooking cashews, date, and water in a saucepan to boil.

Allow it to cool then blend this mixture in a blender until smooth. Spread this icing over the baked cake. Slice and serve.

Nutrition	Calories	184	Fat	9g	Carbs	22g	Protein	4g	Sodium	94mg	Phosphorus	77mg	Potassium	9mg

202. Pumpkin Chocolate Cake

Preparation Time: 10 minutes | Cooking Time: 20 minutes | Servings: 6

Ingredients:

- 2 cups flour
- 1 tablespoon pumpkin pie spice
- 1 teaspoon baking soda
- 2 sticks- 1 cup unsalted butter, softened
- 1-1/4 cup sugar

- 1 egg
- 2 teaspoons vanilla extract
- 1 cup cream cheese
- 1 package 12 oz. chocolate chips

Directions:

Whisk pumpkin pie spice, flour and baking soda in a mixing bowl.

Beat sugar with butter in a mixer until fluffy. Whisk in egg, vanilla, and cream cheese.

Beat well then gradually add the flour mixture while mixing continuously.

Fold in the chocolate chips and grease 2 Bundt pans with cooking oil.

Divide the batter into the pans and cover them with aluminum foil.

Pour 1.5 cups of water into the Instant Pot and place rack over it.

Set one Bundt on the rack and seal the lid. Cook for 20 minutes on Manual mode with High pressure.

Once done, release the pressure completely then remove the lid.

Cook the other cake in the Bundt pan following the same method. Allow the cakes to cool then slice to serve.

Nutrition	Calories	232	Fat	11g	Carbs	30g	Protein	3g	Sodium	46mg	Phosphorus	103mg	Potassium	mg

203. Yummy Lemon Pie

Preparation Time: 25 minutes | Cooking Time: 30 minutes | Servings: 8

Ingredients:

- For the graham cracker crust:
- 1 and 1/2 cups (180 grams) graham cracker crumbs, 11-12 full sheets of graham crackers
- 1/3 cup (65 grams) granulated sugar
- 5 tablespoons (70 grams) unsalted butter, melted and slightly cooled

- For the lemon pie filling:
- 1 cup (240 ml) fresh lemon juice
- 2 (14-ounce) cans sweetened condensed milk
- 5 large egg yolks
- Topping:
- Whipped topping or homemade whipped cream

Directions:

To make the graham cracker crust:

Preheat oven to 350°F.

Combine the graham cracker crumbs and sugar in a mixing bowl and mix until well combined. Add the melted butter and stir until fully combined and all of the crumbs are moistened.

Scoop the mixture into a 9-9.5-inch pie plate and firmly press it down into an even layer on the bottom and up around the sides of the dish.

Bake at 350°F for 8-10 minutes or until the crust is lightly golden brown. Remove from the oven and set aside to cool for 5-10 minutes while you make the filling. Keep oven temperature at 350°F.

<u>To make the lemon pie filling:</u>

Combine the lemon juice, sweetened condensed milk, and egg yolks in a large mixing bowl and whisk until fully combined.

Pour the filling into the slightly cooled graham cracker crust and spread it around into one even layer.

Bake at 350°F for 18-22 minutes or until the top of the pie is set, the pie will still be jiggly.

Remove from the oven and transfer to a wire rack to cool to room temperature for about 2 hours.

Transfer to the refrigerator to chill for at least 5-6 hours or overnight. Once chilled, top with whipped cream, serve and enjoy!

Nutrition	Calories	362	Fat	16.4g	Carbs	49.7g	Protein	4.8g	Sodium	307mg	Phosphorus	109mg	Potassium	207mg

204. Tasty Gumdrop Cookies
Preparation Time: 10 minutes | Cooking Time: 1 hour 30 minutes | Servings: 4

Ingredients:

- 3/4 cup shortening
- 1 cup sugar, divided
- 1/2 teaspoon almond extract
- 1-3/4 cups all-purpose flour
- 1/2 teaspoon baking soda
- 1/4 teaspoon salt
- 1 cup chopped fruit-flavored or spiced gumdrops
- 2 large egg whites

Directions:

Preheat oven to 350°F. Cream shortening and 3/4 cup sugar until light and fluffy.

Beat in almond extract. In another bowl, whisk flour, baking soda and salt; gradually add to creamed mixture and mix well. Stir in gumdrops.

In a separate bowl, beat egg whites until soft peaks form. Gradually add remaining sugar, beating until stiff peaks form. Fold into dough.

Drop by level tablespoonful's 2 in. apart onto ungreased baking sheets.

Bake until golden brown, 12-15 minutes. Cool 1 minute before removing from pans to wire racks to cool completely.

Nutrition	Calories	102	Fat	4g	Carbs	15g	Protein	1g	Sodium	39mg	Phosphorus	57mg	Potassium	99mg

205. Almond Cookies
Preparation Time: 10 minutes | Cooking Time: 35 minutes | Servings: 24

Ingredients:

- 1 tsp cream of tartar
- 2 egg whites or 4 tbsp pasteurized egg whites
- ½ tsp vanilla extract
- ½ tsp almond extract
- ½ cup white sugar

Directions:

Preheat oven to 300°F. Beat egg whites with cream of tartar.

Add remaining ingredients.

Beat until firm peaks are formed.

Push one teaspoon full of meringue onto a parchment-lined cookie sheet with the back of the other spoon.

Bake for approximately 25 minutes or until meringues are crisp.

Nutrition	Calories	184	Fat	9g	Carbs	22g	Protein	4g	Sodium	94mg	Phosphorus	77mg	Potassium	98mg

206. Blueberry and Apple Crisp

Preparation Time: 10 minutes | Cooking Time: 25 minutes | Servings: 8

Ingredients:

- 4 tp cornstarch
- ½ cup brown sugar
- 2 cups grated or chopped apples
- 4 cups of fresh or frozen blueberries (not thawed)
- 1 tbsp lemon juice

- 1 tbsp margarine, melted
- ¼ cup brown sugar
- 1¼ cups quick cooking rolled oats
- 6 tbsp nonhydrogenated margarine, melted
- ¼ cup unbleached all-purpose flour

Directions:

Preheat the oven to 350°F. Combine the dry ingredients in the bowl.

Add butter. Stir until moistened. Set aside.

Combine cornstarch and brown sugar.

Add lemon juice and fruits. Toss.

Top with crisp mixture. Bake for 1 hour until golden brown and serve warm or cold.

Nutrition	Calories	318	Fat	12g	Carbs	52g	Protein	3.3g	Sodium	114mg	Phosphorus	201mg	Potassium	244mg

207. Couscous Pudding

Preparation Time: 10 minutes | Cooking Time: 20 minutes | Servings: 6

Ingredients:

- ½ cup honey
- ¼ teaspoon ground cinnamon
- 1 cup couscous

- 1 ½ cups rice or almond milk
- ½ cup of water
- 1 vanilla bean, split

Directions:

Take a large saucepan or skillet, add milk, water, and vanilla bean. Heat over medium heat.

Over low heat, cover, and simmer the mixture for about 10 minutes for flavor to infuse.

Take off heat and remove vanilla bean.

Scrape seeds from the bean and add back to the mixture.

Add honey and cinnamon. Combine mixture.

Add couscous, stir the mixture, and cover the pan. Set aside for 10 minutes. Serve warm.

Nutrition	Calories	308	Fat	2g	Carbs	63g	Protein	6g	Sodium	64mg	Phosphorus	124mg	Potassium	133mg

208. Egg Custard

Preparation Time: 10 minutes | Cooking Time: 20-30 minutes | Servings: 4

Ingredients:

- 3 tablespoons sugar
- 1 teaspoon vanilla or lemon extract
- 1 teaspoon nutmeg

- 2 medium eggs
- ¼ cup almond or rice milk

Directions:

Preheat an oven to 325°F.

Grease 4 muffin pans or custard cups with some cooking spray.

In a mixing bowl, add all ingredients except nutmeg.

Combine to mix well with each other.

Add the mixture in the pans, sprinkle nutmeg on top, and bake for 20-30 minutes until inserted toothpick comes out clean. Serve warm.

Nutrition	Calories	82	Fat	3g	Carbs	13g	Protein	4g	Sodium	41mg	Phosphorus	46mg	Potassium	34mg

209. Banana Muffins

Preparation Time: 10 minutes | Cooking Time: 12 minutes | Servings: 4

Ingredients:

- 4 tablespoons wheat flour
- 2 bananas, peeled
- 1 tablespoon Plain yogurt
- ½ teaspoon baking powder
- ¼ teaspoon lemon juice
- 1 teaspoon vanilla extract

Directions:

Mash the bananas with the help of the fork.

Then combine mashed bananas with flour, yogurt, baking powder, and lemon juice.

Add vanilla extract and stir the batter until smooth.

Fill ½ part of every muffin mold with banana batter and bake them for 12 minutes at 365°F.

Chill the muffins and remove them from the muffin molds.

Nutrition	Calories	87	Fat	0.3g	Carbs	20.2g	Protein	1.7g	Sodium	46mg	Phosphorus	47mg	Potassium	78mg

210. Grilled Pineapple

Preparation Time: 7 minutes | Cooking Time: 5 minutes | Servings: 4

Ingredients:

- 10 oz fresh pineapple
- ½ teaspoon ground ginger
- 1 tablespoon almond butter, softened

Directions:

Slice the pineapple into the serving pieces and brush with almond butter.

After this, sprinkle every pineapple piece with ground ginger.

Preheat the grill to 400°F.

Grill the pineapple for 2 minutes from each side.

The cooked fruit should have a light brown surface of both sides.

Nutrition	Calories	61	Fat	2.4g	Carbs	10.2g	Protein	1.3g	Sodium	47mg	Phosphorus	67mg	Potassium	78mg

211. Coconut-Mint Bars

Preparation Time: *35 minutes* | ***Cooking Time:*** *1 minutes* | ***Servings:*** *6*

Ingredients:

- 3 tablespoons coconut butter
- ½ cup coconut flakes
- 1 egg, beaten
- 1 tablespoon cocoa powder
- 3 oz graham crackers, crushed
- 2 tablespoons Erythritol
- 3 tablespoons butter
- 1 teaspoon mint extract
- 1 teaspoon stevia powder
- 1 teaspoon of cocoa powder
- 1 tablespoon almond butter, melted

Directions:

Churn together coconut butter, coconut flakes, and 1 tablespoon of cocoa powder.

Then microwave the mixture for 1 minute or until it is melted.

Chill the liquid for 1 minute and fast add egg. Whisk it until homogenous and smooth.

Stir the liquid in the graham crackers and transfer in the mold.

Flatten it well with the help of the spoon.

After this, blend together Erythritol, butter, mint extract, and stevia powder.

When the mixture is fluffy, place it over the graham crackers layer.

Then mix up together 1 teaspoon of cocoa powder and almond butter.

Sprinkle the cooked mixture with cocoa liquid and flatten it.

Refrigerate the dessert for 30 minutes. Then cut it into the bars.

Nutrition	Calories	213	Fat	16.3g	Carbs	20g	Protein	3.5g	Sodium	45mg	Phosphorus	97mg	Potassium	144mg

212. Hummingbird Cake

Preparation Time: *20 minutes* | ***Cooking Time:*** *30 minutes* | ***Servings:*** *10*

Ingredients:

- 1 cup of rice flour
- 1 cup coconut flour
- ½ cup wheat flour
- ½ cup Erythritol
- ½ teaspoon baking powder
- ¾ teaspoon salt
- 1/3 teaspoon ground cinnamon
- ½ cup olive oil
- 2 eggs, beaten
- 3 oz pineapple, chopped
- 1 banana, chopped
- 3 tablespoons walnuts, chopped
- 6 tablespoons cream cheese

Directions:

In the mixing bowl combine together 9 first ingredients from the list above.

When the mixture is smooth and add pineapple and bananas.

Add walnuts and mix up the dough well. Put the dough into the baking pans and bake for 30 minutes at 355°F.

Then remove the cooked cakes from the oven and chill well.

Spread every cake with cream cheese and form them into 1 big cake.

Nutrition	Calories	287	Fat	16g	Carbs	41.9g	Protein	5.5g	Sodium	102mg	Phosphorus	102mg	Potassium	108mg

213. Cool Mango Mousse

Preparation Time: 8 minutes | Cooking Time: 30 minutes | Servings: 6

Ingredients:

- 2 cups coconut cream, chipped
- 6 teaspoons honey
- 2 mangoes, chopped

Directions:

Blend together honey and mango. When the mixture is smooth, combine it with whipped cream and stir carefully.

Put the mango-cream mixture in the serving glasses and refrigerate for 30 minutes.

Nutrition	Calories	272	Fat	19.5g	Carbs	27g	Protein	2.8g	Sodium	49mg	Phosphorus	49mg	Potassium	98mg

214. Sweet Potato Brownies

Preparation Time: 5 minutes | Cooking Time: 30 minutes | Servings: 6

Ingredients:

- 1 tablespoon cocoa powder
- 1 sweet potato, peeled, boiled
- ½ cup wheat flour
- 1 teaspoon baking powder
- 1 tablespoon butter
- 1 tablespoon olive oil
- 2 tablespoons Erythritol

Directions:

In the mixing bowl combine together all ingredients. Mix them well until you get a smooth batter.

After this, pour the brownie batter in the brownie mold and flatten it.

Bake it for 30 minutes at 365°F. After this, cut the brownies into the serving bars.

Nutrition	Calories	95	Fat	4.5g	Carbs	17.8g	Protein	1.6g	Sodium	75mg	Phosphorus	44mg	Potassium	93mg

215. Pumpkin Cookies

Preparation Time: 10 minutes | Cooking Time: 30 minutes | Servings: 6

Ingredients:

- 1 egg, beaten
- 1 teaspoon vanilla extract
- ½ teaspoon ground cinnamon
- 1 teaspoon ground turmeric
- 1 tablespoon butter, softened
- 1 cup wheat flour
- 1 teaspoon baking powder
- 4 tablespoons pumpkin puree
- 1 tablespoon Erythritol

Directions:

Put all ingredients in the mixing bowl and knead the soft and non-sticky dough.

After this, line the baking tray with baking paper. Make 6 balls from the dough and press them gently with the help of the spoon.

Arrange the dough balls in the tray. Bake the cookies for 30 minutes at 355°F. Chill the cooked cookies well and store them in the glass jar.

Nutrition	Calories	111	Fat	2.9g	Carbs	3.2g	Protein	3.2g	Sodium	103mg	Phosphorus	63mg	Potassium	121mg

216. Baked Plums

Preparation Time: 8 minutes | Cooking Time: 20 minutes | Servings: 4

Ingredients:

- 4 plums, pitted, halved, not soft
- 1 tablespoon peanuts, chopp ed
- 1 tablespoon honey
- ½ teaspoon lemon juice
- 1 teaspoon coconut oil

Directions:

Make the packet from the foil and place the plum halves in it.

Then sprinkle the plums with honey, lemon juice, coconut oil, and peanuts. Bake the plums for 20 minutes at 350°F.

Nutrition	Calories	69	Fat	12.9g	Carbs	12.2g	Protein	1.2g	Sodium	61mg	Phosphorus	43mg	Potassium	91mg

217. Classic Parfait

Preparation Time: 10 minutes | Cooking Time: 20 minutes | Servings: 4

Ingredients:

- 1 cup Plain yogurt
- 1 tablespoon coconut flakes
- 1 tablespoon liquid honey
- 4 teaspoons peanuts, chopped
- 1 cup blackberries
- 1 tablespoon pomegranate seeds

Directions:

Mix up together plain yogurt and coconut flakes. Put the mixture in the freezer.

Meanwhile, combine together liquid honey and blackberries.

Place ½ part of blackberry mixture in the serving glasses. Then add ¼ part of the cooled yogurt mixture.

Sprinkle the yogurt mixture with all peanuts and cover with ½ part of remaining yogurt mixture.

Then add remaining blackberries and top the dessert with yogurt. Garnish the parfait with pomegranate seeds and cool in the fridge for 20 minutes.

Nutrition	Calories	115	Fat	3.1g	Carbs	13g	Protein	5.2g	Sodium	37mg	Phosphorus	74mg	Potassium	61mg

218. Melon Popsicles

Preparation Time: 10 minutes | Cooking Time: 2 hours | Servings: 4

Ingredients:

- 9 oz melon, peeled, chopped
- 1 tablespoon Erythritol
- ½ cup of orange juice

Directions:

Blend the melon until smooth and combine it with Erythritol and orange juice.

Mix up the liquid until Erythritol is dissolved. Then pour the liquid into the popsicle's molds.

Freeze the popsicles for 2 hours in the freezer.

Nutrition	Calories	36	Fat	0.2g	Carbs	12.2g	Protein	0.8g	Sodium	41mg	Phosphorus	47mg	Potassium	63mg

219. Watermelon Salad with Shaved Chocolate

*Preparation Time: 10 minutes | **Cooking Time:** 0 minutes | **Servings:** 6*

Ingredients:

- 14 oz watermelon
- 1 oz dark chocolate
- 3 tablespoons coconut cream
- 1 teaspoon Erythritol
- 2 kiwi, chopped
- 1 oz Feta cheese, crumbled

Directions:

Peel the watermelon and remove the seeds from it. Chop the fruit and place in the salad bowl.

Add chopped kiwi and crumbled Feta. Stir the salad well.

Then mix up together coconut cream and Erythritol.

Pour the cream mixture over the salad.

Then shave the chocolate over the salad with the help of the potato peeler. The salad should be served immediately.

Nutrition	Calories	90	Fat	4.4g	Carbs	12.9g	Protein	1.9g	Sodium	74mg	Phosphorus	71mg	Potassium	69mg

220. No-Bake Strawberry Cheesecake

*Preparation Time: 20 minutes | **Cooking Time:** 5 minutes | **Servings:** 8*

Ingredients:

- For Crust:
- 1 cup almonds
- 1 cup pecans
- 2 tablespoons unsweetened coconut flakes
- 6 Medjool dates, pitted, soaked for 10 minutes and drained
- Pinch of salt
- For Filling:
- 3 cups cashews, soaked and drained
- ¼ cup organic honey
- ¼ cup fresh lemon juice
- 1/3 cup coconut oil, melted
- 1 teaspoon organic vanilla flavor
- ¼ teaspoon salt
- 1 cup fresh strawberries, hulled and sliced
- For Topping:
- 1/3 cup maple syrup
- 1/3 cup water
- Drop of vanilla flavor
- 5 cups fresh strawberries, hulled, sliced and divided

Directions:

Grease a 9-inch spring foam pan.

For crust in the small mixer, add almonds and pecans and pulse till finely grounded.

Add remaining all ingredients and pulse till smooth.

Transfer the crust mixture into prepared pan, pressing gently downwards. Freeze to create completely.

In a large blender, add all filling ingredients and pulse till creamy and smooth. Place filling mixture over crust evenly. Freeze for at least couple of hours or till set completely.

In a pan, add maple syrup, water, vanilla and 1 cup of strawberries on medium-low heat.

Bring to a gentle simmer. Simmer for around 4-5 minutes or till thickens.

Strain the sauce and allow it to go cool completely.

Top the chilled cheesecake with strawberry slices. Drizzle with sauce and serve.

Nutrition	Calories	249	Fat	12.1g	Carbs	32g	Protein	5.2g	Sodium	104mg	Phosphorus	32mg	Potassium	120mg

221. Fruity Crumble

Preparation Time: 10 minutes | Cooking Time: 30 minutes | Servings: 6

Ingredients:

- ½ cup unsalted butter
- 1 cup chopped rhubarb
- 1 cup all-purpose flour
- ½ cup brown sugar
- ½ teaspoon cinnamon
- 2 apples, peeled, cored, and thinly sliced
- 2 tablespoons granulated sugar
- 2 tablespoons water

Directions:

Preheat an oven to 325°F. Grease a baking dish (8X8-inch) with some butter.

In a mixing bowl, add flour, sugar, and cinnamon.

Combine to mix well with each other.

Add butter and combine well until your feel coarse crumbs.

Take a medium saucepan or skillet, add rhubarb, apple, sugar, and water. Heat over medium heat for 18-20 minutes until rhubarb is soft.

Pour over baking dish and add crumbs on top.

Bake for 20-30 minutes until golden brown.

Serve warm.

Nutrition	Calories	443	Fat	21g	Carbs	54g	Protein	4g	Sodium	28mg	Phosphorus	61mg	Potassium	193mg

222. Oatmeal Berry Muffins

Preparation Time: 5 minutes | Cooking Time: 30 minutes | Servings: 12

Ingredients:

- ½ cup quick-cooking oatmeal
- 1 cup unbleached all-purpose flour
- ½ tsp baking soda
- ⅔ cup lightly packed brown sugar
- ½ cup applesauce
- 2 eggs
- Zest of 1 orange
- ¼ cup canola oil
- 1 tbsp lemon juice
- Zest of 1 lemon
- ¾ cup blueberries, fresh or frozen
- ¾ cup raspberries, fresh or frozen

Directions:

Preheat the oven to 350°F. Line 12 muffin cups.

Combine baking soda, brown sugar, oatmeal, and flour in a bowl. Set aside.

Whisk lemon juice, applesauce, and eggs in a large bowl.

Stir in the dry ingredients with wooden spoon.

Add the berries. Stir gently.

Scoop into the muffin cups.

Bake for 21 minutes. Let cool.

Nutrition	Calories	173	Fat	5.9g	Carbs	28g	Protein	2.8g	Sodium	49mg	Phosphorus	62mg	Potassium	113mg

223. Berry Fruit Salad with Yogurt

Preparation Time: 10 minutes | Cooking Time: 10 minutes | Servings: 8

Ingredients:

- ¼ cup honey
- 2 cups Greek yogurt
- 1 tbsp lemon juice
- 1 cup blackberries

- 1 cup red cherries, pitted and halved
- 1 cup blueberries
- 1 cup raspberries
- 2 tbsp honey

Directions:

Combine the berries with the honey in a bowl.

Mix the yogurt, lemon juice, and honey in a separate bowl.

Place yogurt cream into the center of each glass. Garnish with the berry fruit salad.

Nutrition	Calories	117	Fat	0.4g	Carbs	27g	Protein	4g	Sodium	28mg	Phosphorus	31mg	Potassium	108mg

224. Sugar Cookie Berry Cups

Preparation Time: 10 minutes | Cooking Time: 30 minutes | Servings: 8

Ingredients:

- 1 roll (16.5 oz) Pillsbury™ refrigerated sugar cookie dough
- 1 cup sugar
- ¼ cup lemon juice
- ¼ cup water
- 3 tablespoons cornstarch

- 1 ½ cups fresh raspberries
- 1 ½ cup fresh blueberries
- 1 ½ cup fresh blackberries
- 1 cup whipped cream (optional)
- 8 sprigs fresh mint leaves for garnish (optional)

Directions:

Preheat oven to 375°F. Spray a standard-sized muffin tin with nonstick baking spray.

Cut the sugar cookie dough into 8 even pieces. Press each piece into the prepared muffin tin, creating a bowl shape in each muffin cup.

Bake sugar cookie cups in preheated oven for 12-15 minutes, or until the center of each cookie has set and the edges are golden brown.

Remove from the oven and tap against the counter a few times to encourage the center of each cup to settle down, creating a space for the berries in the center of each cup.

In a small pot, combine the sugar, lemon juice, water, and cornstarch.

Heat until the mixture is thickened, then allow to cool slightly. Spoon over berries, tossing them gently to coat with the cornstarch and sugar mixture.

Spoon berries into each sugar cookie cup. Garnish with whipped cream and mint springs, if desired.

Nutrition	Calories	315	Fat	15g	Carbs	39g	Protein	3.5g	Sodium	152mg	Phosphorus	82mg	Potassium	141mg

Chapter 9: Smoothies and Drinks

225. Almonds & Blueberries Smoothie

Preparation Time: 5 minutes | Cooking Time: 3 minutes | Servings: 2

Ingredients:

- 1/4 cup ground almonds, unsalted
- 1 cup fresh blueberries
- Fresh juice of a 1 lemon
- 1 cup fresh Kale leaf
- 1/2 cup coconut water
- 1 cup water
- 2 Tbsp plain yogurt (optional)

Directions:

Dump all ingredients in your high-speed blender, and blend until your smoothie is smooth.

Pour the mixture in a chilled glass and serve.

Nutrition	Calories	110	Fat	7g	Carbs	8g	Protein	2g	Sodium	45mg	Phosphorus	31mg	Potassium	73mg

226. Almonds and Zucchini Smoothie

Preparation Time: 5 minutes | Cooking Time: 3 minutes | Servings: 2

Ingredients:

- 1 cup zucchini, cooked and mashed - unsalted
- 1 1/2 cups almond milk
- 1 Tbsp almond butter (plain, unsalted)
- 1 tsp pure almond extract
- 2 Tbsp ground almonds or Macadamia almonds
- 1/2 cup water
- 1 cup Ice cubes crushed (optional, For serving)

Directions:

Dump all ingredients from the list above in your fast-speed blender.

Blend for 45 - 60 seconds or to taste.

Serve with crushed ice.

Nutrition	Calories	322	Fat	30g	Carbs	6g	Protein	6g	Sodium	78mg	Phosphorus	74mg	Potassium	183mg

227. Avocado with Walnut Butter Smoothie

Preparation Time: 5 minutes | Cooking Time: 3 minutes | Servings: 2

Ingredients:

- 1 avocado (diced)
- 1 cup baby spinach
- 1 cup coconut milk (canned)
- 1 Tbsp walnut butter, unsalted
- 2 Tbsp natural sweetener such as Stevia, Erythritol, Truvia...etc.

Directions:

Place all ingredients into food processor or a blender; blend until smooth or to taste.

Add more or less walnut butter.

Drink

Nutrition	Calories	365	Fat	35g	Carbs	7g	Protein	8.3g	Sodium	74mg	Phosphorus	38mg	Potassium	173mg

228. Baby Spinach and Dill Smoothie

Preparation Time: 5 minutes | Cooking Time: 3 minutes | Servings: 2

Ingredients:

- 1 cup of fresh baby spinach leaves
- 2 Tbsp of fresh dill, chopped
- 1 1/2 cup of water
- 1/2 avocado, chopped into cubes
- 1 Tbsp chia seeds (optional)
- 2 Tbsp of natural sweetener Stevia or Erythritol (optional)

Directions:

Place all ingredients into fast-speed blender.

Beat until smooth and all ingredients united well. Serve and enjoy!

Nutrition	Calories	136	Fat	10g	Carbs	8g	Protein	7g	Sodium	28mg	Phosphorus	78mg	Potassium	74mg

229. Blueberries and Coconut Smoothie

Preparation Time: 5 minutes | Cooking Time: 3 minutes | Servings: 5

Ingredients:

- 1 cup of frozen blueberries, unsweetened
- 1 cup Stevia or Erythritol sweetener
- 2 cups coconut milk (canned)
- 1 cup of fresh spinach leaves
- 2 Tbsp shredded coconut (unsweetened)
- 3/4 cup water

Directions:

Place all ingredients from the list in food-processor or in your strong blender.

Blend for 45 - 60 seconds or to taste.

Ready for drink! Serve!

Nutrition	Calories	190	Fat	18g	Carbs	8g	Protein	3g	Sodium	78mg	Phosphorus	19mg	Potassium	43mg

230. Collard Greens and Cucumber Smoothie

Preparation Time: 15 minutes | Cooking Time: 5 minutes | Servings: 2

Ingredients:

- 1 cup Collard greens
- A few fresh pepper mint leaves
- 1 big cucumber
- 1 lime, freshly juiced
- 1/2 cups avocado sliced
- 1 1/2 cup water
- 1 cup crushed ice
- 1/4 cup of natural sweetener Erythritol or Stevia (optional)

Directions:

Rinse and clean your Collard greens from any dirt.

Place all ingredients in a food processor or blender,

Blend until all ingredients in your smoothie is combined well.

Pour in a glass and drink.

Nutrition	Calories	123	Fat	11g	Carbs	8g	Protein	4g	Sodium	45mg	Phosphorus	71mg	Potassium	74mg

231. Creamy Dandelion Greens and Celery Smoothie

Preparation Time: 10 minutes | Cooking Time: 3 minutes | Servings: 2

Ingredients:

- 1 handful of raw dandelion greens
- 2 celery sticks
- 2 Tbsp chia seeds
- 1 small piece of ginger, minced
- 1/2 cup almond milk
- 1/2 cup of water
- 1/2 cup plain yogurt

Directions

Rinse and clean dandelion leaves from any dirt; add in a high-speed blender.

Clean the ginger; keep only inner part and cut in small slices; add in a blender.

Add all remaining ingredient and blend until smooth. Serve and enjoy!

Nutrition	Calories	58	Fat	6g	Carbs	5g	Protein	3g	Sodium	14mg	Phosphorus	25mg	Potassium	73mg

232. Dark Turnip Greens Smoothie

Preparation Time: 10 minutes | Cooking Time: 3 minutes | Servings: 2

Ingredients:

- 1 cup of raw turnip greens
- 1 1/2 cup of almond milk
- 1 Tbsp of almond butter
- 1/2 cup of water
- 1/2 tsp of cocoa powder, unsweetened
- 1 Tbsp of dark chocolate chips
- 1/4 tsp of cinnamon
- A pinch of salt
- 1/2 cup of crushed ice

Directions::

Rinse and clean turnip greens from any dirt. Place the turnip greens in your blender along with all other ingredients.

Blend it for 45 - 60 seconds or until done; smooth and creamy. Serve with or without crushed ice.

Nutrition	Calories	131	Fat	10g	Carbs	5g	Protein	4g	Sodium	28mg	Phosphorus	0.1mg	Potassium	19mg

233. Butter Pecan and Coconut Smoothie

Preparation Time: 5 minutes Cooking Time: 2 minutes Servings: 2

Ingredients:

- 1 cup coconut milk, canned
- 1 scoop Butter Pecan powdered creamer
- 2 cups fresh spinach leaves, chopped
- 1/2 banana frozen or fresh
- 2 Tbsp stevia granulated sweetener to taste
- 1/2 cup water
- 1 cup ice cubes crushed

Directions::

Place ingredients from the list above in your high-speed blender.

Blend for 35 - 50 seconds or until all ingredients combined well. Add less or more crushed ice.

Drink and enjoy!

Nutrition	Calories	268	Fat	26g	Carbs	7g	Protein	4g	Sodium	41mg	Phosphorus	71mg	Potassium	73mg

234. Fresh Cucumber, Kale and Raspberry Smoothie

*Preparation Time: 10 minutes | **Cooking Time:** 3 minutes | **Servings:** 3*

Ingredients:

- 1 1/2 cups of cucumber, peeled
- 1/2 cup raw kale leaves
- 1 1/2 cups fresh raspberries
- 1 cup of almond milk
- 1 cup of water
- Ice cubes crushed (optional)
- 2 Tbsp natural sweetener (Stevia, Erythritol...etc.)

Directions:

Place all ingredients from the list in a food processor or high-speed blender; blend for 35 - 40 seconds.

Serve into chilled glasses.

Add more natural sweeter if you like. Enjoy!

Nutrition	Calories	70	Fat	6g	Carbs	8g	Protein	3g	Sodium	65mg	Phosphorus	13mg	Potassium	45mg

235. Fresh Lettuce and Cucumber-Lemon Smoothie

*Preparation Time: 10 minutes | **Cooking Time:** 3 minutes | **Servings:** 2*

Ingredients:

- 2 cups fresh lettuce leaves, chopped (any kind)
- 1 cup of cucumber
- 1 lemon washed and sliced.
- 1/2 avocado
- 2 Tbsp chia seeds
- 1 1/2 cup water or coconut water
- 1/4 cup stevia granulate sweetener (or to taste)

Directions:

Add all ingredients from the list above in the high-speed blender; blend until completely smooth.

Pour your smoothie into chilled glasses and enjoy!

Nutrition	Calories	51	Fat	4g	Carbs	4g	Protein	2g	Sodium	19mg	Phosphorus	47mg	Potassium	101mg

236. Green Coconut Smoothie

*Preparation Time: 10 minutes | **Cooking Time:** 3 minutes | **Servings:** 2*

Ingredients:

- 1 1/4 cup coconut milk (canned)
- 2 Tbsp chia seeds
- 1 cup of fresh kale leaves
- 1 cup of spinach leaves
- 1 scoop vanilla protein powder
- 1 cup ice cubes
- Granulated stevia sweetener (to taste; optional)
- 1/2 cup water

Directions:

Rinse and clean kale and the spinach leaves from any dirt.

Add all ingredients in your blender.

Blend until you get a nice smoothie. Serve into chilled glass.

Nutrition	Calories	179	Fat	18g	Carbs	5g	Protein	4g	Sodium	19mg	Phosphorus	61mg	Potassium	93mg

237. Instant Coffee Smoothie

Preparation Time: 20 minutes | Cooking Time: 7 minutes | Servings: 2

Ingredients:

- 2 cups of instant coffee
- 1 cup almond milk (or coconut milk)
- 1/4 cup heavy cream
- 2 Tbsp cocoa powder (unsweetened)
- 1 - 2 Handful of fresh spinach leaves
- 10 drops liquid stevia

Directions:

Make a coffee; set aside.

Place all remaining ingredients in your fast-speed blender; blend for 45 - 60 seconds or until done.

Pour your instant coffee in a blender and continue to blend for further 30 - 45 seconds. Serve immediately.

Nutrition	Calories	142	Fat	14g	Carbs	6g	Protein	5g	Sodium	46mg	Phosphorus	35mg	Potassium	73mg

238. Keto Blood Sugar Adjuster Smoothie

Preparation Time: 10 minutes | Cooking Time: 3 minutes | Servings: 2

Ingredients:

- 2 cups of green cabbage
- 1/2 avocado
- 1 Tbsp Apple cider vinegar
- Juice of 1 small lemon
- 1 cup of water
- 1 cup of crushed ice cubes For serving

Directions:

Place all ingredients in your high-speed blender or in a food processor and blend until smooth and soft.

Serve in chilled glasses with crushed ice.

Nutrition	Calories	74	Fat	6g	Carbs	7g	Protein	2g	Sodium	19mg	Phosphorus	61mg	Potassium	13mg

239. Cinnamon Egg Smoothie

Preparation Time: 10 minutes | Cooking Time: 0 minutes | Servings: 4

Ingredients:

- 1/2 teaspoon ground cinnamon
- 1 teaspoon stevia
- 1/8 teaspoon vanilla extract
- 8 oz. egg white, pasteurized
- 3 tablespoons whipped topping

Directions:

Mix the stevia, egg whites, cinnamon, and vanilla in a mixer. Serve with whipped topping.

Nutrition	Calories	95	Fat	1.2g	Carbs	3.4g	Protein	14g	Sodium	120mg	Phosphorus	185mg	Potassium	193mg

240. Pineapple Sorbet Smoothie

Preparation Time: 10 minutes | Cooking Time: 0 minutes | Servings: 4

Ingredients:

- 3/4 cup pineapple sorbet
- 1 scoop protein powder
- 1/2 cup water
- 2 ice cubes, optional

Directions:

First, begin by putting everything into a blender jug.

Pulse it for 30 seconds until well blended.

Serve chilled.

Nutrition	Calories	180	Fat	1g	Carbs	34g	Protein	13g	Sodium	86mg	Phosphorus	164mg	Potassium	113mg

241. Vanilla Fruit Smoothie

Preparation Time: 10 minutes | Cooking Time: 0 minutes | Servings: 4

Ingredients:

- 2 oz. mango, peeled and cubed
- 2 oz. strawberries
- 2 oz. avocado flesh, cubed
- 2 oz. banana, peeled
- 2 scoops of protein powder
- 1 cup cold water
- 1 cup crushed ice

Directions:

First, begin by putting everything into a blender jug.

Pulse it for 30 seconds until well blended. Serve chilled.

Nutrition	Calories	228	Fat	7.6g	Carbs	19g	Protein	23.4g	Sodium	58mg	Phosphorus	216mg	Potassium	503mg

242. Protein Berry Smoothie

Preparation Time: 10 minutes | Cooking Time: 0 minutes | Servings: 4

Ingredients:

- 4 oz. water
- 1 cup frozen mixed berries
- 2 ice cubes
- 1 teaspoon blueberry essence
- 2 scoops whey protein powder

Directions:

First, begin by putting everything into a blender jug.

Pulse it for 30 seconds until well blended. Serve chilled.

Nutrition	Calories	248	Fat	11.4g	Carbs	13.3g	Protein	23.3g	Sodium	67mg	Phosphorus	156mg	Potassium	293mg

243. Raspberry Peach Smoothie

Preparation Time: 5 minutes | Cooking Time: 0 minutes | Servings: 3

Ingredients:

- 1 medium peach, sliced
- 1 cup frozen raspberries
- 1 tablespoon honey
- ½ cup tofu
- 1 cup unfortified almond milk

Directions:

Mix all the ingredients in your blender. Serve chilled.

Nutrition	Calories	129	Fat	3.2g	Carbs	23g	Protein	6.3g	Sodium	69mg	Phosphorus	161mg	Potassium	203mg

244. Blueberry Smoothie

Preparation Time: 5 minutes | Cooking Time: 0 minutes | Servings: 3

Ingredients:

- 2 cups frozen blueberries (slightly thawed)
- 1 ¼ cup pineapple juice
- 2 tsp sugar or Splenda
- ¾ cup pasteurized egg whites
- ½ cup water

Directions:

Mix all the ingredients in blender and puree. Serve chilled.

Nutrition	Calories	155	Fat	0.8g	Carbs	31g	Protein	7.4g	Sodium	48mg	Phosphorus	171mg	Potassium	193mg

245. Cinnamon Apple Water

Preparation Time: 5 minutes | Cooking Time: 0 minutes | Servings: 10

Ingredients:

- 1 medium apple, thinly sliced
- 10 cups water
- 2 tsp ground cinnamon
- 2 cinnamon sticks

Directions:

Put all ingredients in a pitcher. Refrigerate overnight and serve.

Nutrition	Calories	4	Fat	0.1g	Carbs	0.9g	Protein	0g	Sodium	0mg	Phosphorus	1.2mg	Potassium	13mg

246. Apple and Beet Juice Mix

Preparation Time: 5 minutes | Cooking Time: 0 minutes | Servings: 2

Ingredients:

- ½ medium beet
- ½ medium apple
- 1 celery stalk
- 1 medium fresh carrot
- ¼ cup parsley

Directions:

Juice all ingredients. Pour the mixture in 2 glasses and serve

Nutrition	Calories	53	Fat	0g	Carbs	13g	Protein	1g	Sodium	12mg	Phosphorus	41mg	Potassium	13mg

247. Protein Caramel Latte

Preparation Time: 4 minutes | Cooking Time: 10 minutes | Servings: 1

Ingredients:

- 0,5 cups ounces of water
- 1 scoop whey protein powder
- 2 tbsp of Caramel Sugar-Free Syrup
- 6 ounces hot coffee

Directions:

Combine protein powder and water. Stir in coffee and caramel syrup.

Nutrition	Calories	72	Fat	0g	Carbs	1.3g	Protein	17g	Sodium	19mg	Phosphorus	19mg	Potassium	103mg

248. Protein Peach Smoothie

Preparation Time: 4 minutes | Cooking Time: 0 minutes | Servings: 1

Ingredients:

- 1/2 cup ice
- 2 tablespoons egg whites, pasteurized
- 3/4 cup fresh peaches
- 1 teaspoon stevia

Directions:

First, begin by putting everything into a blender jug. Pulse it for 30 seconds until well blended. Serve chilled.

Nutrition	Calories	195	Fat	0.2g	Carbs	17g	Protein	24.3g	Sodium	347mg	Phosphorus	233mg	Potassium	526mg

249. Cranberry Cucumber Smoothie

Preparation Time: 4 minutes | Cooking Time: 0 minutes | Servings: 1

Ingredients:

- 1 cup frozen cranberries
- 1 medium cucumber, peeled and sliced
- 1 stalk of celery
- 1 teaspoon lime juice

Directions:

First, begin by putting everything into a blender jug. Pulse it for 30 seconds until well blended. Serve chilled.

Nutrition	Calories	119	Fat	0.2g	Carbs	25.1g	Protein	2.3g	Sodium	21mg	Phosphorus	184mg	Potassium	325mg

250. Creamy Dandelion Greens and Celery Smoothie

Preparation Time: 4 minutes | Cooking Time: 0 minutes | Servings: 1

Ingredients:

- 1 handful of raw dandelion greens
- 2 celery sticks
- 2 Tbsp chia seeds
- 1 small piece of ginger, minced
- 1/2 cup almond milk
- 1/2 cup of water
- 1/2 cup plain yogurt

Directions:

Rinse and clean dandelion leaves from any dirt; add in a high-speed blender.

Clean the ginger; keep only inner part and cut in small slices; add in a blender. Add all remaining ingredients and blend until smooth. Serve.

Nutrition	Calories	58	Fat	6g	Carbs	5.2g	Protein	3g	Sodium	38mg	Phosphorus	171mg	Potassium	253mg

251. Dark Turnip Greens Smoothie

Preparation Time: 4 minutes | Cooking Time: 0 minutes | Servings: 1

Ingredients:

- 1 cup of raw turnip greens
- 1 1/2 cup of almond milk
- 1 Tbsp of almond butter
- 1/2 cup of water
- 1/2 tsp of cocoa powder, unsweetened
- 1 Tbsp of dark chocolate chips
- 1/4 tsp of cinnamon
- A pinch of salt
- 1/2 cup of crushed ice

132

Directions:

Rinse and clean turnip greens from any dirt. Place the turnip greens in your blender along with all other Ingredients.

Blend it for 45 - 60 seconds or until done; smooth and creamy. Serve with or without crushed ice.

Nutrition	Calories	131	Fat	10g	Carbs	6g	Protein	6g	Sodium	31mg	Phosphorus	111mg	Potassium	147mg

252. Butter Pecan and Coconut Smoothie

Preparation Time: 4 minutes | Cooking Time: 0 minutes | Servings: 1

Ingredients:

- 1 cup coconut milk, canned
- 1 scoop Butter Pecan powdered creamer
- 2 cups fresh spinach leaves, chopped
- 1/2 banana frozen or fresh
- 2 Tbsp stevia granulated sweetener to taste
- 1/2 cup water
- 1 cup ice cubes crushed

Directions:

Place Ingredients from the list above in your high-speed blender. Blend for 35 - 50 seconds or until all Ingredients combined well. Add less or more crushed ice. Drink and enjoy!

Nutrition	Calories	268	Fat	26g	Carbs	7g	Protein	6g	Sodium	71mg	Phosphorus	74mg	Potassium	102mg

253. Fresh Cucumber, Kale and Raspberry Smoothie

Preparation Time: 4 minutes | Cooking Time: 0 minutes | Servings: 1

Ingredients:

- 1 1/2 cups of cucumber, peeled
- 1/2 cup raw kale leaves
- 1 1/2 cups fresh raspberries
- 1 cup of almond milk
- 1 cup of water
- Ice cubes crushed (optional)
- 2 Tbsp natural sweetener (Stevia, Erythritol...etc.)

Directions:

Place all Ingredients from the list in a food processor or high-speed blender; blend for 35 - 40 seconds. Serve into chilled glasses. Add more natural sweeter if you like.

Nutrition	Calories	70	Fat	6g	Carbs	7g	Protein	3g	Sodium	47mg	Phosphorus	95mg	Potassium	32mg

254. Fresh Lettuce and Cucumber-Lemon Smoothie

Preparation Time: 4 minutes | Cooking Time: 0 minutes | Servings: 1

Ingredients:

- 2 cups fresh lettuce leaves, chopped (any kind)
- 1 cup of cucumber
- 1 lemon, washed and sliced.
- 1/2 avocado
- 2 Tbsp chia seeds
- 1 1/2 cup water or coconut water
- 1/4 cup stevia granulate sweetener (or to taste)

Directions:

Add all Ingredients from the list above in the high-speed blender; blend until completely smooth. Pour your smoothie into chilled glasses and enjoy!

Nutrition	Calories	51	Fat	4g	Carbs	4g	Protein	3g	Sodium	63mg	Phosphorus	120mg	Potassium	142mg

255. Green Coconut Smoothie

Preparation Time: 4 minutes | Cooking Time: 0 minutes | Servings: 1

Ingredients:

- 1 1/4 cup coconut milk (canned)
- 2 Tbsp chia seeds
- 1 cup of fresh kale leaves
- 1 cup of spinach leaves
- 1 scoop vanilla protein powder
- 1 cup ice cubes
- Granulated stevia sweetener (to taste; optional)
- 1/2 cup water

Directions:

Rinse and clean kale and the spinach leaves from any dirt.

Add all Ingredients in your blender.

Blend until you get a nice smoothie.

Serve into chilled glass.

Nutrition	Calories	179	Fat	18g	Carbs	5g	Protein	4g	Sodium	79mg	Phosphorus	104mg	Potassium	189mg

256. Instant Coffee Smoothie

Preparation Time: 4 minutes | Cooking Time: 0 minutes | Servings: 1

Ingredients:

- 2 cups of instant coffee
- 1 cup almond milk (or coconut milk)
- 1/4 cup heavy cream
- 2 Tbsp cocoa powder (unsweetened)
- 1 - 2 Handful of fresh spinach leaves
- 10 drops liquid stevia

Directions:

Make a coffee; set aside.

Place all remaining ingredients in your fast-speed blender; blend for 45 - 60 seconds or until done.

Pour your instant coffee in a blender and continue to blend for further 30 - 45 seconds.

Serve immediately.

Nutrition	Calories	142	Fat	14g	Carbs	6g	Protein	5g	Sodium	102mg	Phosphorus	104mg	Potassium	152mg

257. Keto Blood Sugar Adjuster Smoothie

Preparation Time: 4 minutes Cooking Time: 0 minutes Servings: 1

Ingredients:

- 2 cups of green cabbage
- 1/2 avocado
- 1 Tbsp Apple cider vinegar
- Juice of 1 small lemon
- 1 cup of water
- 1 cup of crushed ice cubes For serving

Directions:

Place all ingredients in your high-speed blender or in a food processor and blend until smooth and soft.

Serve in chilled glasses with crushed ice.

Nutrition	Calories	74	Fat	6g	Carbs	7g	Protein	2g	Sodium	19mg	Phosphorus	65mg	Potassium	122mg

258. Raspberry Smoothie

Preparation Time: 4 minutes | Cooking Time: 0 minutes | Servings: 1

Ingredients:

- 1 cup frozen raspberries
- 1 medium peach, pitted, sliced
- ½ cup tofu
- 1 tablespoon honey
- 1 cup milk

Directions:

First, begin by putting everything into a blender jug. Pulse it for 30 seconds until well blended.

Serve chilled.

Nutrition	Calories	233	Fat	2.6g	Carbs	49.9g	Protein	3.6g	Sodium	99mg	Phosphorus	95mg	Potassium	426mg

259. Citrus Pineapple Shake

Preparation Time: 4 minutes | Cooking Time: 0 minutes | Servings: 1

Ingredients:

- 1/2 cup pineapple juice
- 1/2 cup almond milk
- 1 cup orange sherbet
- 1/2 cup egg, pasteurized

Directions:

Pour the almond milk, pineapple juice, sherbet, and egg into the blender. Blend well for 1 minute then refrigerate to chill.

Serve.

Nutrition	Calories	242	Fat	8.2g	Carbs	33g	Protein	8.9g	Sodium	155mg	Phosphorus	121mg	Potassium	234mg

260. Pineapple Smoothie

Preparation Time: 4 minutes | Cooking Time: 0 minutes | Servings: 1

Ingredients:

- 3/4 cup pineapple sherbet
- 1 scoop protein powder
- 1/2 cup water
- 2 ice cubes

Directions:

Add the water, pineapple sherbet, protein powder, and ice to a blender. Blend the pineapple smoothie for 1 minute.

Serve.

Nutrition	Calories	91	Fat	0.6g	Carbs	10.4g	Protein	11.6g	Sodium	361mg	Phosphorus	49mg	Potassium	25mg

261. Hazelnut Coffee

Preparation Time: 4 minutes | Cooking Time: 10 minutes | Servings: 1

Ingredients:

- 4 cups brewed coffee
- 8 teaspoons hazelnut syrup
- 4 tablespoons almond milk
- 8 cinnamon sticks

Directions:

Begin by brewing the coffee in a coffee maker, then pour it into the 4 small serving cups.

Add 1 tablespoon almond milk, 2 teaspoons hazelnut syrup, and 2 cinnamon sticks to each mug. Serve.

Nutrition	Calories	65	Fat	4.5g	Carbs	4.7g	Protein	2.6g	Sodium	24mg	Phosphorus	73mg	Potassium	302mg

262. Lemon Piña Colada

Preparation Time: 4 minutes | Cooking Time: 0 minutes | Servings: 1

Ingredients:

- 6 oz. pineapple juice
- 1 oz. lemon-lime juice
- 1 oz. protein powder
- 1/2 cup crushed ice
- 2 slices fresh pineapple

Directions:

Put the protein powder, pineapple juice, and ice into a blender jug.

Pour the piña colada mixture into the serving glasses. Top the Piña Coladas with lemon-lime juice.

Garnish with pineapple slices. Serve.

Nutrition	Calories	227	Fat	2.2g	Carbs	31.7g	Protein	21.6g	Sodium	60mg	Phosphorus	94mg	Potassium	462mg

263. Blueberry Apple Blast

Preparation Time: 4 minutes | Cooking Time: 0 minutes | Servings: 1

Ingredients:

- 1 cup frozen blueberries
- 6 tablespoons vanilla protein powder
- 8 ice cubes
- 14 oz. apple juice

Directions:

First, begin by putting everything into a blender jug. Pulse it for 30 seconds until well blended. Serve chilled.

Nutrition	Calories	260	Fat	2.3g	Carbs	338.8g	Protein	23g	Sodium	71mg	Phosphorus	105mg	Potassium	495mg

264. Allspice Cider

Preparation Time: 4 minutes | Cooking Time: 0 minutes | Servings: 1

Ingredients:

- 8 cups apple cider
- 3 cinnamon sticks
- 1/4 teaspoon whole cloves
- 1/4 teaspoon ground allspice

Directions:

Add the cider, cinnamon sticks, allspice, and cloves to a slow cooker. Cook this apple cider mixture for 1 hour on low heat. Strain and serve.

Nutrition	Calories	118	Fat	0.3g	Carbs	29.3g	Protein	0.2g	Sodium	8mg	Phosphorus	124mg	Potassium	298mg

Chapter 10: Salads

265. Italian Cucumber Salad

Preparation Time: *5 minutes* | ***Cooking Time:*** *0 minutes* | ***Servings:*** *2*

Ingredients:

- 1/4 cup rice vinegar
- 1/8 teaspoon stevia
- 1/2 teaspoon olive oil
- 1/8 teaspoon black pepper
- 1/2 cucumber, sliced
- 1 cup carrots, sliced
- 2 tablespoons green onion, sliced
- 2 tablespoons red bell pepper, sliced
- 1/2 teaspoon Italian seasoning blend

Directions:

Put all the salad ingredients into a suitable salad bowl. Toss them well and refrigerate for 1 hour. Serve.

Nutrition	Calories	112	Fat	1.6	Carbs	8.3g	Protein	2.9g	Sodium	43mg	Phosphorus	198mg	Potassium	529mg

266. Grapes Jicama Salad

Preparation Time: *5 minutes* | ***Cooking Time:*** *0 minutes* | ***Servings:*** *2*

Ingredients:

- 1 jicama, peeled and sliced
- 1 carrot, sliced
- 1/2 medium red onion, sliced
- 1 ¼ cup seedless grapes
- 1/3 cup fresh basil leaves
- 1 tablespoon apple cider vinegar
- 1 ½ tablespoon lemon juice
- 1 ½ tablespoon lime juice

Directions:

Put all the salad ingredients into a suitable salad bowl. Toss them well and refrigerate for 1 hour. Serve.

Nutrition	Calories	203	Fat	0.7g	Carbs	48.2g	Protein	3.7g	Sodium	44mg	Phosphorus	141mg	Potassium	429mg

267. Cucumber Couscous Salad

Preparation Time: *5 minutes* | ***Cooking Time:*** *0 minutes* | ***Servings:*** *4*

Ingredients:

- 1 cucumber, sliced
- ½ cup red bell pepper, sliced
- ¼ cup sweet onion, sliced
- 2 tablespoons black olives, sliced
- ¼ cup parsley, chopped
- ½ cup couscous, cooked
- 2 tablespoons olive oil
- 2 tablespoons rice vinegar
- 2 tablespoons feta cheese crumbled
- 1 ½ teaspoon dried basil
- 1/4 teaspoon black pepper

Directions:

Put all the salad ingredients into a suitable salad bowl.

Toss them well and refrigerate for 1 hour.

Serve.

Nutrition	Calories	202	Fat	9.8g	Carbs	22.4g	Protein	6.2g	Sodium	258mg	Phosphorus	192mg	Potassium	209mg

268. Carrot Jicama Salad

Preparation Time: 10 minutes | Cooking Time: 0 minutes | Servings: 2

Ingredients:

- 2 cup carrots, julienned
- 1 1/2 cups jicama, julienned
- 2 tablespoons lime juice
- 1 tablespoon olive oil
- ½ tablespoon apple cider
- ½ teaspoon brown Swerve

Directions:

Put all the salad ingredients into a suitable salad bowl.

Toss them well and refrigerate for 1 hour.

Serve.

Nutrition	Calories	173	Fat	7.1g	Carbs	20.7g	Protein	1.6g	Sodium	80mg	Phosphorus	96mg	Potassium	501mg

269. Butterscotch Apple Salad

Preparation Time: 8 minutes | Cooking Time: 0 minutes | Servings: 6

Ingredients:

- 3 cups jazz apples, chopped
- 8 oz. canned crushed pineapple
- 8 oz. whipped topping
- 1/2 cup butterscotch topping
- 1/3 cup almonds
- 1/4 cup butterscotch chips

Directions:

Put all the salad ingredients into a suitable salad bowl.

Toss them well and refrigerate for 1 hour.

Serve.

Nutrition	Calories	293	Fat	12.7g	Carbs	45.5g	Protein	4.2g	Sodium	152mg	Phosphorus	202mg	Potassium	296mg

270. Cranberry Cabbage Slaw

Preparation Time: 8 minutes | Cooking Time: 0 minutes | Servings: 4

Ingredients:

- 1/2 medium cabbage head, shredded
- 1 medium red apple, shredded
- 2 tablespoons onion, sliced
- 1/2 cup dried cranberries
- 1/4 cup almonds, toasted sliced
- 1/2 cup olive oil
- ¼ teaspoon stevia
- 1/4 cup cider vinegar
- 1/2 tablespoon celery seed
- 1/2 teaspoon dry mustard
- ½ cup cream

Directions:

Take a suitable salad bowl.

Start tossing in all the ingredients.

Mix well and serve.

Nutrition	Calories	308	Fat	24g	Carbs	13.5g	Protein	2.6g	Sodium	23mg	Phosphorus	257mg	Potassium	217mg

271. Chestnut Noodle Salad

Preparation Time: 10 minutes | Cooking Time: 0 minutes | Servings: 6

Ingredients:

- 8 cups cabbage, shredded
- 1/2 cup canned chestnuts, sliced
- 6 green onions, chopped
- 1/4 cup olive oil
- 1/4 cup apple cider vinegar
- 3/4 teaspoon stevia
- 1/8 teaspoon black pepper
- 1 cup chow Mein noodles, cooked

Directions:

Take a suitable salad bowl. Start tossing in all the ingredients. Mix well and serve.

Nutrition	Calories	191	Fat	13g	Carbs	5.8g	Protein	4.2g	Sodium	78mg	Phosphorus	188mg	Potassium	302mg

272. Cranberry Broccoli Salad

Preparation Time: 10 minutes | Cooking Time: 0 minutes | Servings: 4

Ingredients:

- 3/4 cup plain Greek yogurt
- 1/4 cup mayonnaise
- 2 tablespoons maple syrup
- 2 tablespoons apple cider vinegar
- 4 cups broccoli florets
- 1 medium apple, chopped
- 1/2 cup red onion, sliced
- 1/4 cup parsley, chopped
- 1/2 cup dried cranberries
- 1/4 cup pecans

Directions:

Put all the salad ingredients into a suitable salad bowl.

Toss them well and refrigerate for 1 hour.

Serve.

Nutrition	Calories	252	Fat	10.5g	Carbs	34g	Protein	9.4g	Sodium	157mg	Phosphorus	291mg	Potassium	480mg

273. Balsamic Beet Salad

Preparation Time: 10 minutes | Cooking Time: 0 minutes | Servings: 2

Ingredients:

- 1 cucumber, peeled and sliced
- 15 oz. canned low-sodium beets, sliced
- 4 teaspoon balsamic vinegar
- 2 teaspoon sesame oil
- 2 tablespoons Gorgonzola cheese

Directions:

Take a suitable salad bowl.

Start tossing in all the ingredients.

Mix well and serve.

Nutrition	Calories	145	Fat	7.8g	Carbs	16.4g	Protein	5g	Sodium	426mg	Phosphorus	79mg	Potassium	229mg

274. Shrimp Salad

Preparation Time: 8 minutes | Cooking Time: 0 minutes | Servings: 4

Ingredients:

- 1 lb. shrimp, boiled and chopped
- 1 hardboiled egg, chopped
- 1 tablespoon celery, chopped
- 1 tablespoon green pepper, chopped
- 1 tablespoon onion, chopped
- 2 tablespoons mayonnaise

- 1 teaspoon lemon juice
- ½ teaspoon chili powder
- ⅛ teaspoon hot sauce
- ½ teaspoon dry mustard
- Lettuce, chopped or shredded

Directions:

Take a suitable salad bowl.

Start tossing in all the ingredients.

Mix well and serve.

Nutrition	Calories	184	Fat	5.7g	Carbs	4.3g	Protein	27.5g	Sodium	381mg	Phosphorus	249mg	Potassium	233mg

275. Chicken Cranberry Sauce Salad

Preparation Time: 10 minutes | Cooking Time: 0 minutes | Servings: 6

Ingredients:

- 3 cups of chicken meat, cooked, cubed
- 1 cup grapes
- 2 cups carrots, shredded
- 1/4 red onion, chopped

- 1 large yellow bell pepper, chopped
- 1/4 cup mayonnaise
- 1/2 cup cranberry sauce

Directions:

Put all the salad ingredients into a suitable salad bowl.

Toss them well and refrigerate for 1 hour.

Serve.

Nutrition	Calories	240	Fat	8.6g	Carbs	19.4g	Protein	21g	Sodium	161mg	Phosphorus	260mg	Potassium	260mg

276. Egg Celery Salad

Preparation Time: 10 minutes | Cooking Time: 0 minutes | Servings: 4

Ingredients:

- 4 eggs, boiled, peeled and chopped
- 1/4 cup celery, chopped
- 1/2 cup sweet onion, chopped

- 2 tablespoons sweet pickle, chopped
- 3 tablespoons mayonnaise
- 1 tablespoon mustard

Directions:

Put all the salad ingredients into a suitable salad bowl.

Toss them well and refrigerate for 1 hour.

Serve.

Nutrition	Calories	134	Fat	8.9g	Carbs	7.4g	Protein	6.8g	Sodium	259mg	Phosphorus	357mg	Potassium	112mg

277. Chicken Orange Salad

Preparation Time: 10 minutes | Cooking Time: 0 minutes | Servings: 4

Ingredients:

- 1 ½ cup chicken, cooked and diced
- ½ cup celery, diced
- ½ cup green pepper, chopped
- ¼ cup onion, sliced

- 1 cup orange, peeled and cut into segments
- ¼ cup mayonnaise
- ½ teaspoon black pepper

Directions:

Take a suitable salad bowl.

Start tossing in all the ingredients.

Mix well and serve.

Nutrition	Calories	167	Fat	6.7g	Carbs	11.2g	Protein	16g	Sodium	151mg	Phosphorus	211mg	Potassium	242mg

278. Almond Pasta Salad

Preparation Time: 10 minutes | Cooking Time: 0 minutes | Servings: 14

Ingredients:

- 1 lb. elbow macaroni, cooked
- 1/2 cup sun-dried tomatoes, diced
- 1 (15 oz.) can whole artichokes, diced
- 1 orange bell pepper, diced
- 3 green onions, sliced
- 2 tablespoons basil, sliced
- 2 oz. slivered almonds

- Dressing:
- 1 garlic clove, minced
- 1 tablespoon Dijon mustard
- 1 tablespoon raw honey
- 1/4 cup white balsamic vinegar
- 1/3 cup olive oil

Directions:

Take a suitable salad bowl.

Start tossing in all the ingredients.

Mix well and serve.

Nutrition	Calories	260	Fat	7.7g	Carbs	41.2g	Protein	9.6g	Sodium	143mg	Phosphorus	39mg	Potassium	585mg

279. Pineapple Berry Salad

Preparation Time: 10 minutes | Cooking Time: 0 minutes | Servings: 4

Ingredients:

- 4 cups pineapple, peeled and cubed
- 3 cups strawberries, chopped
- 1/4 cup honey

- 1/2 cup basil leaves
- 1 tablespoon lemon zest
- 1/2 cup blueberries

Directions:

Take a suitable salad bowl.

Start tossing in all the ingredients. Mix well and serve.

Nutrition	Calories	128	Fat	0.6g	Carbs	33.1g	Protein	1.8g	Sodium	3mg	Phosphorus	151mg	Potassium	362mg

280. Lettuce and Carrot Salad with Balsamic Vinaigrette

Preparation Time: 25 minutes | Cooking Time: 0 minutes | Servings: 4

Ingredients:

- For the vinaigrette
- Olive oil – ½ cup
- Balsamic vinegar - 4 tbsp
- Chopped fresh oregano – 2 tbsp
- Pinch red pepper flakes
- Ground black pepper

- For the salad
- Shredded green leaf lettuce – 4 cups
- Carrot – 1, shredded
- Fresh green beans – ¾ cup, cut into 1-inch pieces
- Large radishes – 3, sliced thinly

Directions:

To make the vinaigrette: place the vinaigrette ingredients in a bowl and whisk.

To make the salad: in a bowl, toss together the carrot, lettuce, green beans, and radishes.

Add the vinaigrette to the vegetables and toss to coat.

Arrange the salad on plates and serve.

Nutrition	Calories	237	Fat	27g	Carbs	7g	Protein	1g	Sodium	27mg	Phosphorus	30mg	Potassium	197mg

281. Strawberry Watercress Salad with Almond Dressing

Preparation Time: 15 minutes | Cooking Time: 0 minutes | Servings: 6

Ingredients:

- For the dressing
- Olive oil – ¼ cup
- Rice vinegar – ¼ cup
- Honey – 1 tbsp
- Pure almond extract – ¼ tsp
- Ground mustard – ¼ tsp
- Ground black pepper

- For the salad
- Chopped watercress – 2 cups
- Shredded green leaf lettuce – 2 cups
- Red onion – ½, sliced very thin
- English cucumber – ½, chopped
- Sliced strawberries – 1 cup

Directions:

To make the dressing, in a small bowl, whisk together the olive oil and rice vinegar until mixed.

Whisk in the almond extract, honey, mustard, and pepper. Set aside.

To make the salad: In a large bowl, toss together the watercress, green leaf lettuce, onion, cucumber, and strawberries.

Pour the dressing over the salad and toss to combine.

Nutrition	Calories	159	Fat	14g	Carbs	9g	Protein	1g	Sodium	14mg	Phosphorus	34mg	Potassium	195mg

282. Cucumber and Cabbage Salad with Lemon Dressing

Preparation Time: 25 minutes | Cooking Time: 0 minutes | Servings: 4

Ingredients:

- Heavy cream – ¼ cup
- Freshly squeezed lemon juice – ¼ cup
- Granulated sugar – 2 tbsp
- Chopped fresh dill – 2 tbsp

- Finely chopped scallion – 2 tbsp, green part only
- Ground black pepper – ¼ tsp
- English cucumber – 1, sliced thinly
- Shredded green cabbage – 2 cups

Directions:

In a small bowl, stir together the lemon juice, cream, sugar, dill, scallion, and pepper until well blended.

In a large bowl, toss together the cucumber and cabbage.

Place the salad in the refrigerator and chill for 1 hour.

Stir before serving.

Nutrition	Calories	99	Fat	6g	Carbs	13g	Protein	2g	Sodium	14mg	Phosphorus	38mg	Potassium	200mg

283. Lettuce, Asparagus and Raspberries Salad

Preparation Time: 25 minutes | Cooking Time: 0 minutes | Servings: 4

Ingredients:

- Shredded green leaf lettuce – 2 cups
- Asparagus – 1 cup, cut into long ribbons with a peeler
- Scallion – 1, both green and white parts, sliced
- Raspberries – 1 cup
- Balsamic vinegar – 2 tbsp
- Ground black pepper to taste

Directions:

Arrange the lettuce evenly on 4 serving plates.

Arrange the asparagus and scallion on top of the greens.

Place the raspberries on top of the salads, dividing the berries evenly.

Drizzle the salads with balsamic vinegar.

Season with pepper.

Nutrition	Calories	36	Fat	0g	Carbs	8g	Protein	2g	Sodium	11mg	Phosphorus	43mg	Potassium	11mg

284. Waldorf Salad with Variation

Preparation Time: 20 minutes | Cooking Time: 0 minutes | Servings: 4

Ingredients:

- Green leaf lettuce - 3 cups, torn into pieces
- Halved grapes – 1 cup
- Celery stalks – 3, chopped
- Apple – 1, chopped
- Light sour cream – ½ cup
- Freshly squeezed lemon juice – 2 tbsp
- Granulated sugar – 1 tbsp

Directions:

Arrange the lettuce evenly on 4 plates. Set aside.

In a bowl, stir together the grapes, celery, and apple.

In another bowl, stir together the sour cream, lemon juice, and sugar.

Add the sour cream mixture to the grape mixture and stir to coat.

Spoon the dressed grape mixture onto each plate, dividing the mixture evenly.

Nutrition	Calories	73	Fat	2g	Carbs	15g	Protein	1g	Sodium	30mg	Phosphorus	29mg	Potassium	194mg

285. Asian Pear Salad

Preparation Time: 30 minutes | Cooking Time: 0 minutes | Servings: 6

Ingredients:

- Shredded green cabbage – 2 cups
- Shredded red cabbage – 1 cup
- Scallions – 2, both green and white parts, chopped
- Celery stalks -2, chopped
- Asian pear - 1, cored and grated
- Red bell pepper – ½, boiled and chopped
- Chopped cilantro – ½ cup
- Olive oil – ¼ cup
- Juice of 1 lime
- Zest of 1 lime
- Granulated sugar – 1 tsp

Directions:

In a bowl, toss together the green and red cabbage, scallions, celery, pear, red pepper, and cilantro.

In a bowl, whisk together the olive oil, lime juice, lime zest, and sugar.

Add the dressing to the cabbage mixture and toss to coat. Chill for 1 hour and serve.

Nutrition	Calories	105	Fat	9g	Carbs	6g	Protein	1g	Sodium	48mg	Phosphorus	17mg	Potassium	136mg

286. Couscous Salad with Spicy Citrus Dressing

Preparation Time: 25 minutes | Cooking Time: 0 minutes | Servings: 6

Ingredients:

- For the dressing
- Olive oil – ¼ cup
- Grapefruit juice – 3 tbsp.
- Juice of 1 lime
- Zest of 1 lime
- Chopped fresh parsley – 1 tbsp.
- Pinch cayenne pepper
- Ground black pepper
- For the salad
- Cooked couscous – 3 cups, chilled
- Red bell pepper – ½, chopped
- Scallion – 1, both white and green parts, chopped
- Apple – 1, chopped

Directions:

To make the dressing, in a bowl, whisk together the grapefruit juice, olive oil, lime juice, lime zest, parsley, and cayenne pepper.

Season with black pepper.

To make the salad, in a bowl, mix the red pepper, chilled couscous, scallion, and apple.

Add the dressing to the couscous mixture and toss to combine. Chill in the refrigerator and serve.

Nutrition	Calories	187	Fat	9g	Carbs	23g	Protein	3g	Sodium	5mg	Phosphorus	24mg	Potassium	108mg

287. Farfalle Confetti Salad

Preparation Time: 30 minutes | Cooking Time: 0 minutes | Servings: 6

Ingredients:

- Cooked farfalle pasta – 2 cups
- Boiled and finely chopped red bell pepper – ¼ cup
- Finely chopped cucumber – ¼ cup
- Grated carrot – ¼ cup
- Yellow bell pepper – 2 tbsp
- Scallion – ½, green part only, finely chopped
- Homemade mayonnaise – ½ cup
- Freshly squeezed lemon juice – 1 tbsp
- Chopped fresh parsley – 1 tsp
- Granulated sugar – ½ tsp
- Freshly ground black pepper

144

Directions:

In a bowl, toss together the pasta, red pepper, carrot, cucumber, yellow pepper, and scallion.

In a bowl, whisk together the mayonnaise, parsley, lemon juice, and sugar.

Add the dressing to the pasta mixture and stir to combine.

Season with pepper. Chill for 1 hour and serve.

Nutrition	Calories	119	Fat	3g	Carbs	20g	Protein	4g	Sodium	16mg	Phosphorus	51mg	Potassium	82mg

288. Tarragon and Pepper Pasta Salad
Preparation Time: 10 minutes | Cooking Time: 35 minutes | Servings: 4

Ingredients:

- Cooked pasta – 2 cups
- Red bell pepper – 1, finely diced
- Cucumber – ½, finely diced
- Red onion – ¼, finely diced
- Black pepper – 1 tsp
- Extra virgin olive oil – 2 tbsp
- Dried tarragon – 1 tbsp

Directions:

Cook pasta according to package

Cool and combine the rest of the raw ingredients and mix well.

Serve.

Nutrition	Calories	157	Fat	8g	Carbs	24g	Protein	11g	Sodium	5mg	Phosphorus	61mg	Potassium	95mg

289. Zucchini and Crispy Salmon Salad
Preparation Time: 2 minutes | Cooking Time: 15 minutes | Servings: 2

Ingredients:

- Skinless salmon fillets – 2 (3 oz. each)
- Spinach – ½ cup
- Zucchini – ½ cup, sliced
- Balsamic vinegar – 1 tbsp
- Extra virgin olive oil – 2 tbsp
- Thyme – 2 sprigs, torn
- Lemon – 1 juiced

Directions:

Preheat the broiler to medium-high heat.

Cook the salmon in parchment paper with 1 tbsp. oil, lemon, and pepper for 10 minutes.

Remove the parchment paper and finish under the broiler for 5 minutes until golden brown and crispy. Remove.

Heat 1 tbsp. oil in a pan on medium heat.

Add the zucchini slices and sauté for 5 to 6 minutes.

Add the spinach to the pan and allow to wilt for 30 seconds.

Add the salmon fillets to a bed of zucchini and spinach, and drizzle with balsamic vinegar and a sprinkle of thyme.

Nutrition	Calories	309	Fat	23g	Carbs	5g	Protein	22g	Sodium	52mg	Phosphorus	294mg	Potassium	118mg

290. Brie and Apple Salad

Preparation Time: 5 minutes | Cooking Time: 0 minutes | Servings: 2

Ingredients:

- Brie – ½ cup, sliced
- Apple – ½, peeled, cored and diced
- Watercress – 1 cup
- White vinegar - 1 tsp

Directions:

Toss watercress in vinegar and scatter with brie and apple. Serve with Melba toast or crackers.

Nutrition	Calories	111	Fat	7g	Carbs	8g	Protein	5g	Sodium	7mg	Phosphorus	20mg	Potassium	99mg

291. Macaroni Tuna Salad

Preparation Time: 5 minutes | Cooking Time: 25 minutes | Servings: 8

Ingredients:

- 1 (170 g) can of tuna (white flaked or solid) packed in water
- 1½ cups uncooked macaroni
- 2 celery stalks, diced
- ¼ c mayonnaise
- 1 tsp lemon pepper seasoning

Directions:

Cook pasta. Chill in the fridge. Remove water from tuna. Rinse in a colander.

Combine celery, tuna, and macaroni when it has cooled.

Stir in lemon pepper and mayonnaise. Serve chilled.

Nutrition	Calories	136	Fat	3.6g	Carbs	18g	Protein	8g	Sodium	49mg	Phosphorus	91mg	Potassium	142mg

292. Beef Salad

Preparation Time: 15 minutes | Cooking Time: 35 minutes | Servings: 12

Ingredients:

- 8 cups torn romaine lettuce
- ½ cup each julienned cucumber, sweet yellow pepper, and red onion
- 4 tsp canola oil
- ½ cup of halved grape tomatoes
- Chili-Lime Vinaigrette
- ¼ cup fresh lime juice
- 1 tsp of grated lime rind
- 1 tbsp honey
- 1 tbsp Asian chili sauce
- 2 tbsp rice vinegar
- 1 tbsp minced ginger root
- 1 tbsp fresh lime juice
- 1 tbsp cornstarch
- 1 tsp sesame oil
- 1 tsp Asian chili sauc
- 2 cloves garlic, minced
- 1 lb Beef Strip Loin, Top Sirloin or Flank Steak, thinly sliced

Directions:

Combine the chili sauce, sesame oil, garlic, lime juice, ginger root, and cornstarch in a medium bowl.

Add beef. Toss to coat. Let stand for 10 minutes.

In a large frypan, heat 1 tsp canola oil.

Stir-fry onion, yellow pepper, cucumber, tomatoes until just wilted and hot. Transfer to the clean bowl.

Heat the remaining canola oil in same pan. Stir-fry beef until cooked and browned.

Add to wilted vegetables, tossing to combine.

Whisk all Chili-Lime Vinaigrette ingredients together.

Put Chili-Lime Vinaigrette in the pan. Cook until hot and slightly thickened. Top romaine with veggies and beef and vinaigrette.

Nutrition	Calories	116	Fat	6g	Carbs	6g	Protein	13g	Sodium	71mg	Phosphorus	147mg	Potassium	242mg

293. Beet Feta Salad

Preparation Time: 10 minutes | Cooking Time: 30 minutes | Servings: 5

Ingredients:

- 4 cups baby salad greens
- ½ sweet onion, sliced
- 8 small beets, trimmed
- 2 tablespoons + 1 teaspoon extra-virgin olive oil
- 1 tablespoon white wine vinegar
- 1 teaspoon Dijon mustard
- Black pepper (ground), to taste
- 2 tablespoons crumbled feta cheese
- 2 tablespoons walnut pieces

Directions:

Preheat an oven to 400⁰F. Grease an aluminum foil with some cooking spray.

Add beets with 1 teaspoon of olive oil; combine and wrap foil.

Bake for 30 minutes until it becomes tender. Cut beets into wedges.

In a mixing bowl, add remaining olive oil, vinegar, black pepper, and mustard. Combine to mix well with each other.

In a mixing bowl, add salad greens, onion, feta cheese, and walnuts.

Combine to mix well with each other.

Add half of the prepared vinaigrette and toss well. Add beet and combine well.

Drizzle remaining vinaigrette and serve fresh.

Nutrition	Calories	184	Fat	9g	Carbs	19g	Protein	4g	Sodium	235mg	Phosphorus	98mg	Potassium	235mg

294. Cabbage Pear Salad

Preparation Time: 1 hour and 5 minutes | Cooking Time: 0 minutes S| ervings: 6

Ingredients:

- 2 scallions, chopped
- 2 cups finely shredded green cabbage
- 1 cup finely shredded red cabbage
- ½ red bell pepper, boiled and chopped
- ½ cup chopped cilantro
- 2 celery stalks, chopped
- 1 Asian pear, cored and grated
- ¼ cup olive oil
- Juice of 1 lime
- Zest of 1 lime
- 1 teaspoon granulated sugar

Directions:

In a mixing bowl, add cabbages, scallions, celery, pear, red pepper, and cilantro. Combine to mix well with each other.

Take another mixing bowl; add olive oil, lime juice, lime zest, and sugar. Combine to mix well with each other.

Add dressing over and toss well. Refrigerate for 1 hour and serve chilled.

Nutrition	Calories	128	Fat	8g	Carbs	2g	Protein	6g	Sodium	57mg	Phosphorus	25mg	Potassium	149mg

295. Strawberry Zippy Salad

Preparation Time: 5 minutes | Cooking Time: 10 minutes | Servings: 6

Ingredients:

- Salad:
- ½ cup slivered almonds, toasted
- 10 cups torn salad greens
  2 cups sliced strawberries
- 1 cup grapes, halved
  2 cups mandarin orange segments
- ½ cup crushed, unsalted pretzels

- Dressing:
- ⅓ cup white wine vinegar
- ½ cup vegetable oil
  2 tbsp brown sugar
- 1 garlic clove, minced
  1 tsp low sodium soy sauce
- 1 tsp curry powder

Directions:

Combine all the salad ingredients in a bowl.

Combine all the dressing ingredients in a sealed container. Shake well.

Toss salad with dressing and serve.

Nutrition	Calories	256	Fat	18g	Carbs	24g	Protein	4g	Sodium	47mg	Phosphorus	89mg	Potassium	172mg

296. Creamed Chicken Salad

Preparation Time: 20 minutes + chilling time | Cooking Time: 15 minutes | Servings: 4

Ingredients:

- 2 chicken breasts, skinless and boneless
- 1 teaspoon Dijon mustard
- 2 teaspoons freshly squeezed lemon juice

- 1 cup mayonnaise, preferably homemade
- 4 scallions, trimmed and thinly sliced

Directions:

Place the chicken in a stockpot; cover with water by 1 inch and bring to a boil.

Then, continue to simmer for 13 to 16 minutes (a meat thermometer should read 165°F).

When cool enough to handle, cut the chicken into strips and place them in a serving bowl.

Toss the chicken with the remaining ingredients.

Serve with fresh coriander if desired.

Nutrition	Calories	536	Fat	3.1g	Carbs	3.9g	Protein	19g	Sodium	105mg	Phosphorus	112mg	Potassium	195mg

297. Couscous Salad

Preparation Time: 5 minutes | Cooking Time: 5 minutes | Servings: 12

Ingredients:

- ½ tsp cinnamon
- 3 cups water
- 1 tbsp honey
- ½ tsp cumin
- 3 cups of quick-cooking couscous
- 2 tbsp lemon juice

- 1 green onion finely chopped
- 2 tsp olive oil
- ½ red pepper finely chopped
- 1 small carrot finely chopped
- 1 cup of fresh cilantro

Directions:

Bring water to boil with lemon juice, honey, cumin, and cinnamon.

Add couscous and cook according to package instructions.

Fluff with a fork.

Add fresh herbs, olive oil, and veggies.

Serve either chilled or warm.

Nutrition	Calories	190	Fat	1g	Carbs	38g	Protein	6g	Sodium	61mg	Phosphorus	71mg	Potassium	102mg

298. Arugula Parmesan Salad

Preparation Time: 10 minutes | Cooking Time: 0 minutes | Servings: 4

Ingredients:

- 2 cups loosely packed arugula
- 1 tablespoon extra-virgin olive oil
- 1 shallot, thinly sliced
- 3 celery stalks, cut into 1-inch pieces about ¼ inch thick
- 2 tablespoons white wine vinegar
- Black pepper (ground), to taste
- 2 tablespoons Parmesan cheese, grated

Directions:

In a mixing bowl, add shallot, celery stalks, and arugula. Combine to mix well with each other.

Take another mixing bowl; add olive oil, vinegar, and black pepper. Combine to mix well with each other.

Add dressing over and toss well.

Add cheese on top and serve fresh.

Nutrition	Calories	61	Fat	4g	Carbs	1g	Protein	2g	Sodium	55mg	Phosphorus	34mg	Potassium	53mg

299. Eggplant Bean Rice Meal

Preparation Time: 10 minutes | Cooking Time: 20 minutes | Servings: 6

Ingredients:

- 1 tablespoon grated fresh ginger
- 2 teaspoons minced garlic
- 1 tablespoon olive oil
- ½ sweet onion, chopped
- 1 cup sliced carrots
- ½ cup green beans, cut into 1-inch pieces
- 2 tablespoons fresh cilantro, chopped
- 3 cups cooked rice
- ½ cup chopped eggplant
- ½ cup peas

Directions:

Take a medium saucepan or skillet, add oil. Heat over medium heat.

Add onion and stir-cook until become translucent and softened about 2 minutes.

Add garlic, ginger, and stir-cook until become fragrant.

Add veggies; stir-cook for 3 minutes more.

Add cilantro and rice; stir-cook for 8-10 minutes more until rice is cooked well. Serve warm.

Nutrition	Calories	204	Fat	6g	Carbs	26g	Protein	6g	Sodium	33mg	Phosphorus	98mg	Potassium	185mg

300. Coleslaw

*Preparation Time: 5 minutes | **Cooking Time:** 7 minutes | **Servings:** 8*

Ingredients:

- ¼ cup canola oil
- ¼ cup mayonnaise
- 1 small cabbage, chopped
- 1 large carrot, grated
- 3 tbsp sugar

Directions:

Mix all ingredients and serve chilled.

Nutrition	Calories	136	Fat	9.6g	Carbs	12.6g	Protein	1.3g	Sodium	79mg	Phosphorus	211mg	Potassium	242mg

Conclusion

You likely had little knowledge about your kidneys before. You probably didn't know how you could take steps to improve your kidney health and decrease the risk of developing kidney failure. However, through reading this book, you now understand the power of the human kidney, as well as the prognosis of chronic kidney disease. While over thirty-million Americans are being affected by kidney disease, you can now take steps to be one of the people who is actively working to promote your kidney health. Kidney disease now ranks as the 18th deadliest condition in the world. In the United States alone, it is reported that over 600,000 Americans succumb to kidney failure.

These stats are alarming, which is why, it is necessary to take proper care of your kidneys, starting with a kidney-friendly diet. These recipes are ideal whether you have been diagnosed with a kidney problem or you want to prevent any kidney issue. With regards to your wellbeing and health, it's a smart thought to see your doctor as frequently as conceivable to ensure you don't run into preventable issues that you needn't get. The kidneys are your body's toxin channel (just like the liver), cleaning the blood of remote substances and toxins that are discharged from things like preservatives in food & other toxins. At the point when you eat flippantly and fill your body with toxins, either from nourishment, drinks (liquor or alcohol for instance) or even from the air you inhale (free radicals are in the sun and move through your skin, through messy air, and numerous food sources contain them). Your body additionally will in general convert numerous things that appear to be benign until your body's organs convert them into things like formaldehyde because of a synthetic response and transforming phase.

One case of this is a large portion of those diet sugars utilized in diet soft drinks for instance, Aspartame transforms into Formaldehyde in the body. These toxins must be expelled, or they can prompt ailment, renal (kidney) failure, malignant growth, & various other painful problems.

This isn't a condition that occurs without any forethought it is a dynamic issue and in that it very well may be both found early and treated, diet changed, and settling what is causing the issue is conceivable. It's conceivable to have partial renal failure yet, as a rule; it requires some time (or downright awful diet for a short time) to arrive at absolute renal failure. You would prefer not to reach total renal failure since this will require standard dialysis treatments to save your life. Dialysis treatments explicitly clean the blood of waste and toxins in the blood utilizing a machine in light of the fact that your body can no longer carry out the responsibility. Without treatments, you could die a very painful death. Renal failure can be the consequence of long-haul diabetes, hypertension, unreliable diet, and can stem from other health concerns. A renal diet is tied in with directing the intake of protein and phosphorus in your eating routine. Restricting your sodium intake is likewise significant. By controlling these two variables you can control the vast majority of the toxins/waste made by your body and thus this enables your kidney to 100% function. In the event that you get this early enough and truly moderate your diets with extraordinary consideration, you could avert all-out renal failure. In the event that you get this early, you can take out the issue completely.

Printed in Great Britain
by Amazon

58336802R00086